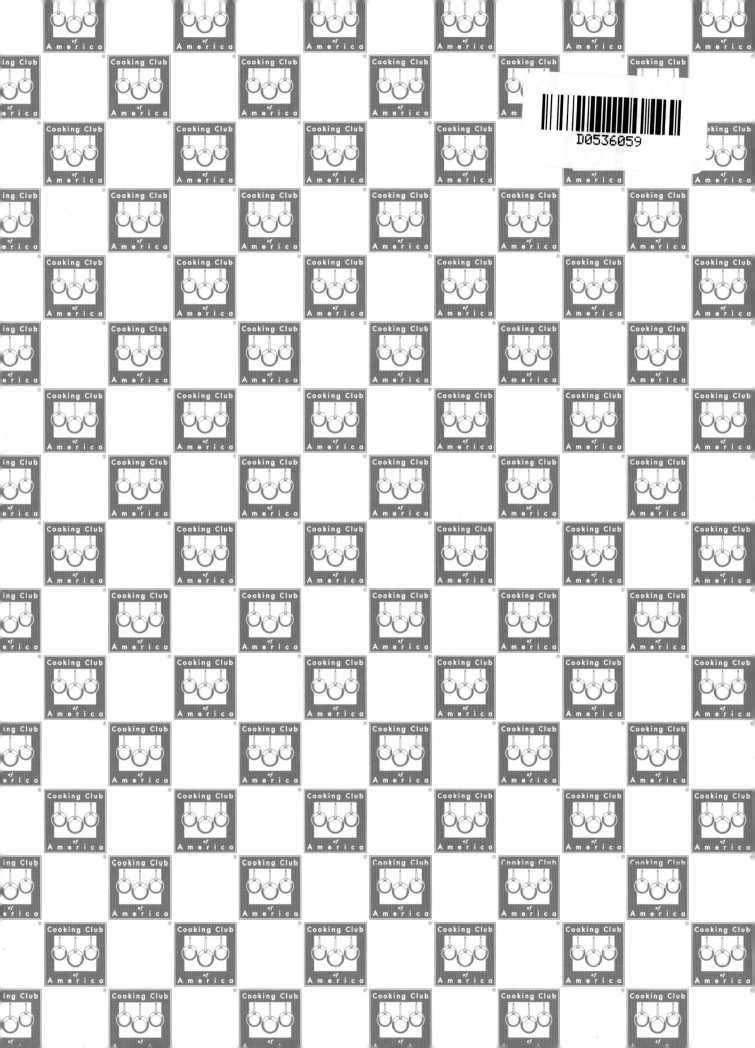

YOU DESERVE DESSERT!

Member Recipes

Cooking Club
of
America

You Deserve DESSERT!

Wacky Cake with Caramel Icing (page 13)

Tom Carpenter
Creative Director

Jennifer Weaverling
Senior Book Development Coordinator

Laura Holle
Book Development Assistant

Zachary Marell
Book Design and Production

Lisa Golden Schroeder
Recipe Editor and Food Stylist

Mowers Photography
Commissioned Photography

Peter Bischoff
Photo Assistant

Kimberly Colburn
Pegi Lee
Assistant Food Stylists

On Cover: Raspberry Pie, page 32.
On Page 1: Wine Braised Pear Chantilly, page 133.

8 9 10 11 12 / 09 08 07 06
© 2000 Cooking Club of America
ISBN 1-58159-120-9

Cooking Club of America
12301 Whitewater Drive
Minnetonka, MN 55343
www.cookingclub.com

The Cooking Club of America proudly presents this special cookbook edition which includes the personal favorites of your fellow Members. Each recipe has been screened by a cooking professional and edited for clarity; most were kitchen tested. However, we are not able to kitchen-test every recipe and cannot guarantee their outcome, or your safety in their preparation or consumption. Please be advised that any recipes which require the use of dangerous equipment (such as pressure cookers) or potentially unsafe preparation procedures (such as canning and pickling), should be used with caution and safe, healthy practices.

Double Chocolate Fudge Cake (page 109)

Mini Cheesecakes (page 128)

CONTENTS

Frozen Pudding Sandwiches (page 144)

Go Ahead ... You Deserve DESSERT!

Since we were little, we've heard all about the foods that are good for us: milk for strong bones and teeth, carrots for sharp eyes, protein-rich meat to build muscles, pasta and breads for energy. Most of us can recite many more items from that long list.

But there's one glaring absence from the litany of "good for you" things, one important food item that never really qualified for the list: dessert. No kidding!

How can *dessert* be good for someone? What does dessert take care of in the scheme of things? Simple. Dessert just makes you feel good ... an important food for the soul, a little break from reality and rules.

Yes, there's usually sugar involved, which of course means some calories. But if it tastes great, you love eating it and it makes you feel good, what's wrong with something sweet—a little dessert—now and again? You deserve it.

Those were our simple sentiments as we at the Cooking Club of America created this book. And when it came time to name the pages you're holding, we thought why not call it like we see it: *You Deserve DESSERT!*

Grandma Betty's Upside-Down Cobbler (page 37)

Crème De Menthe Brownies with a Crust (page 85)

You can thank your fellow members for this book. They're the ones that provided recipes by the hundreds. In fact, the hardest part about our job was whittling down all those submissions into the 253-recipe package you're holding. Not an easy task!

You'll find it all here—awesome items for dessert, and goodies and sweets beyond the dinner table. Great cakes for occasions casual and fancy. Pies and cobblers. Cookies, bars and brownies. Puddings and custards and other creamy creations. Cheesecakes and many other special desserts. Ice creams, and sauces to go with them. Plus candies, confections and other sweet treats.

This may not be a cookbook you pull out and use every day, and that's fine. But it *is* a resource of ideas that will keep you creating wonderful desserts—and feeling good about them—for a long time to come.

You work hard, and love to cook. Don't shy away from one of the foods you love that also makes you happy. You deserve DESSERT!

GREAT CAKES &

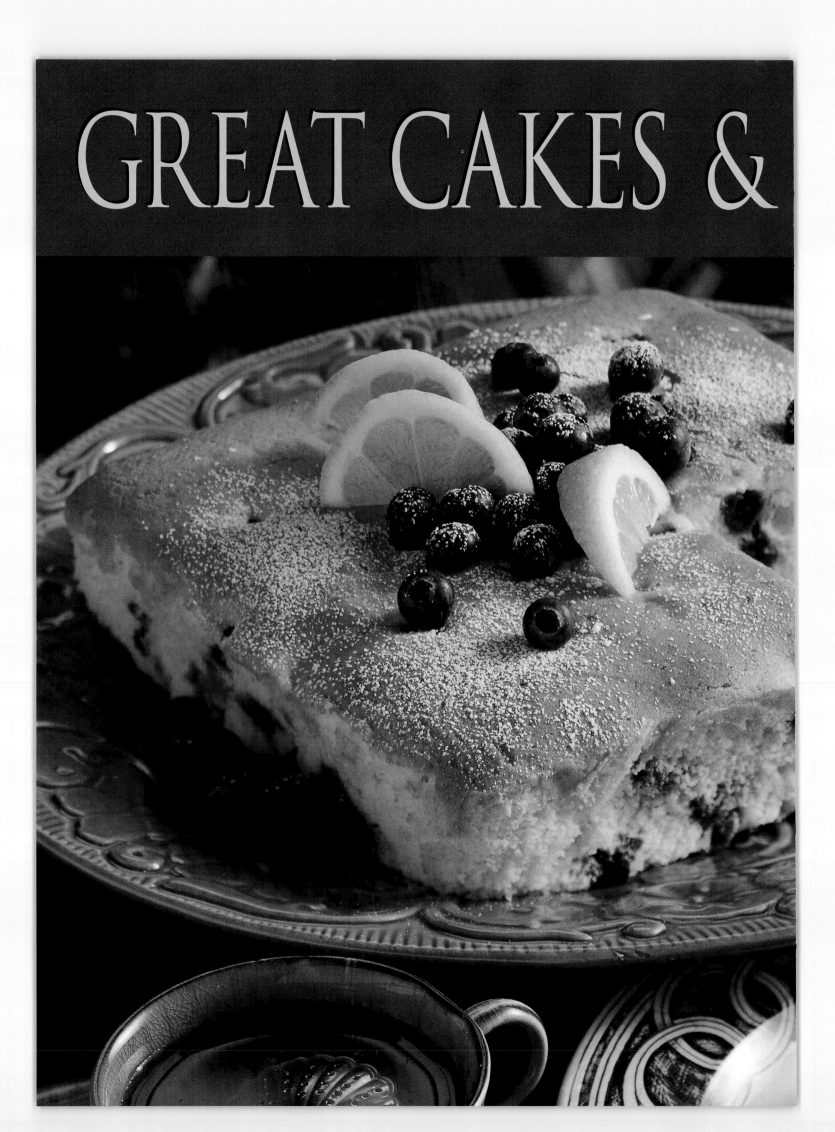

SWEET BREADS

BLUEBERRY TEA CAKE
WITH LEMON SAUCE (page 16)

VOLCANO CAKE

RANDEE ECKSTEIN
LITTLE NECK, NEW YORK

CAKE

2 1/2 cups all-purpose flour

1 1/2 cups sugar

1/2 cup unsweetened cocoa

2 teaspoons baking soda

1/2 teaspoon salt

2/3 cup vegetable oil

2 tablespoons apple cider vinegar

1 tablespoon vanilla

2 cups cold coffee

TOPPING

1/3 cup sugar

1 teaspoon cinnamon

1 Heat oven to 350°F. Stir together flour, 1 1/2 cups sugar, cocoa, baking soda and salt. Make 3 depressions in dry mixture. Pour oil into one depression, cider vinegar into another, and vanilla into third depression. Pour coffee over entire surface; mix well.

2 Spread evenly in 13x9-inch pan. In small bowl, stir 1/3 cup sugar and cinnamon together; sprinkle one-half of topping over cake.

3 Bake 30 to 40 minutes or until toothpick inserted in center comes out clean. Sprinkle with remaining topping. Cool 20 minutes before serving.

16 servings

GINGERBREAD WITH HOT FUDGE SAUCE

KAY SPARKMAN
ALEXANDRIA, VIRGINIA

BREAD

1/2 cup butter, softened

1/2 cup sugar

2 eggs

1 cup molasses

2 cups all-purpose flour

1 teaspoon ground ginger

1 teaspoon cinnamon

1 teaspoon ground cloves

1 teaspoon salt

1 teaspoon baking soda

1 cup hot water

SAUCE

2 (1-oz.) squares unsweetened chocolate

1 tablespoon butter

1/3 cup boiling water

2 tablespoons light corn syrup

1/3 cup sugar

1 teaspoon vanilla

1 Heat oven to 350°F. Spray 9-inch round cake pan with nonstick cooking spray.

2 In large bowl, beat 1/2 cup butter and 1/2 cup sugar at medium-high speed until fluffy. Add eggs; beat well. Add molasses; beat well.

3 In another large bowl, mix flour, ginger, cinnamon, cloves and salt. Dissolve baking soda in 1 cup hot water. Gradually add and stir in flour mixture alternately with water and soda, starting and ending with dry ingredients. Pour into pan.

4 Bake 30 minutes or until toothpick inserted in center comes out clean. Cool in pan on wire rack.

5 To prepare sauce, melt chocolate and 1 tablespoon butter with 1/3 cup water in medium saucepan over medium heat; stir until smooth. Add syrup and 1/3 cup sugar. Increase heat to medium-high, stirring occasionally until boiling. Reduce heat to medium-low. Allow mixture to simmer exactly 8 minutes without stirring. Dip saucepan briefly in cold water. Stir in vanilla. Serve warm over gingerbread with vanilla ice cream, if desired. Store in refrigerator.

8 servings

MISSISSIPPI MUD CAKE

LENA RICE
BOISE, IDAHO

CAKE

2 cups sugar

1 cup vegetable oil

4 eggs

1 1/2 cups all-purpose flour

1/3 cup unsweetened cocoa

1/4 teaspoon salt

2 teaspoons vanilla

3/4 cup chopped nuts

1 (7-oz.) jar marshmallow crème

TOPPING

1/2 cup butter, melted

1/2 cup unsweetened cocoa

1 (16-oz.) pkg. powdered sugar

1/2 cup evaporated milk

1 teaspoon vanilla

3/4 cup chopped nuts

1 Heat oven to 350°F. Spray 13x9-inch pan with nonstick cooking spray.

2 In large bowl, cream sugar and oil. Add eggs and beat at medium speed until light and fluffy. Add flour, 1/3 cup cocoa and salt; beat well. Add 2 teaspoons vanilla, 3/4 cup nuts and marshmallow crème; beat well. Pour mixture into pan.

3 Bake 30 minutes. Cool cake in pan on wire rack until set or about 10 minutes.

4 To prepare topping, combine butter, 1/2 cup cocoa, powdered sugar, evaporated milk, 1 teaspoon vanilla and 3/4 cup chopped nuts in large bowl. Beat at medium speed until smooth. With spatula, spread topping over cake. Store in refrigerator.

16 servings

GREEK NUT CAKE

VASSIE SEMI
LA MESA, CALIFORNIA

CAKE

2 cups buttermilk baking mix

1 cup pecans or walnuts, coarsely chopped

1 cup sugar

1 1/2 teaspoons baking powder

1 teaspoon cinnamon

1/4 teaspoon ground cloves

1/2 teaspoon ground nutmeg

4 eggs

3/4 cup milk

3/4 cup vegetable oil

TOPPING

1 1/2 cups sugar

1 1/4 cups water

2 teaspoons grated orange peel

1 Heat oven to 375°F. Spray 9-inch round cake pan with nonstick cooking spray.

2 In large bowl, stir together baking mix, nuts, 1 cup sugar, baking powder, cinnamon, cloves, nutmeg, eggs, milk and oil until blended. Pour into pan.

3 Bake 30 minutes or until toothpick inserted in center comes out clean.

4 To prepare topping, heat 1 1/2 cups sugar, water and orange peel in medium saucepan over high heat. Bring to a boil. Boil 2 minutes; remove from heat. Let stand until cake is finished baking.

5 Immediately spoon topping over cake. Cool cake in pan on wire rack.

8 servings

HONEY-NUT POUND CAKE

JOHN F. WILLIAMS, SR.
BEAUMONT, TEXAS

1/2 cup butter, softened

1 cup packed brown sugar

2 eggs

2 tablespoons honey

1 1/2 cups cake flour

1/2 teaspoon baking powder

1/4 teaspoon baking soda

1/2 cup buttermilk

2 teaspoons vanilla

1 cup coarsely chopped pecans

1 Heat oven to 350°F. Spray 9x5-inch loaf pan with nonstick cooking spray.

2 In large bowl, beat butter and sugar at medium-high speed until fluffy. Add eggs, one at a time, mixing thoroughly after each addition. Stir in honey.

3 In large bowl, sift together flour, baking powder and baking soda. Gradually add and stir in flour mixture to sugar mixture alternately with buttermilk, ending with buttermilk. Stir in vanilla. Fold 3/4 cup of the chopped pecans into batter. Spoon batter into pan. Sprinkle remaining 1/4 cup pecans on top.

4 Bake 50 to 55 minutes or until toothpick inserted in center comes out clean. Cool in pan on wire rack. Store in refrigerator.

12 servings

CHOCOLATE-CHERRY CAKE

DOROTHY H. JOHNSON
HECTOR, MINNESOTA

CAKE

2/3 cup butter

2 cups sugar

2 eggs

2 (1-oz.) squares unsweetened chocolate, melted

2 cups all-purpose flour

2 teaspoons baking soda

1 teaspoon salt

1 (8-oz.) jar maraschino cherries, drained, juice reserved, cut up

Buttermilk to make 2 cups liquid

ICING

6 tablespoons butter

6 tablespoons milk

1 1/2 cups sugar

1 teaspoon vanilla

1/2 cup semisweet chocolate chips

1 Heat oven to 350°F. Spray 13x9-inch pan with nonstick cooking spray.

2 In large bowl, beat 2/3 cup butter and 2 cups sugar at medium-high speed until fluffy. Add eggs and chocolate; beat well.

3 In another large bowl, mix together flour, baking soda and salt. To reserved cherry juice, add enough buttermilk to make 2 cups. Add buttermilk mixture alternately with flour to batter, mixing well. Fold in cherries. Pour into pan.

4 Bake 1 hour or until toothpick inserted in center comes out clean. Cool cake in pan on wire rack.

5 To prepare icing, in large saucepan, heat remaining 6 tablespoons butter, milk and 1 1/2 cups sugar to a boil; boil 30 seconds. Remove from heat; add vanilla and chocolate chips. Beat by hand 3 minutes. Spread icing over cooled cake.

8 servings

TEXAS SHEET CAKE

KITTI BOESEL
GLEN BURNIE, MARYLAND

1/2 cup unsweetened cocoa

1 1/2 cups butter

1 cup water

2 cups sugar

2 cups all-purpose flour

1/2 teaspoon salt

1 cup sour cream

1 teaspoon baking soda

2 eggs

2 teaspoons vanilla

1 teaspoon cinnamon

6 tablespoons milk

1 (16-oz.) pkg. powdered sugar

1 Heat oven to 375°F. Spray 15 1/2x10 1/2x1-inch baking pan with nonstick cooking spray.

2 Heat 1/4 cup of the cocoa, 1 cup of the butter, and water to boiling in small saucepan over high heat; remove from heat. Stir in sugar, flour and salt. Beat in sour cream, baking soda, eggs, 1 teaspoon of the vanilla and cinnamon at medium speed 1 minute or until blended, scraping bowl occasionally. Pour into pan.

3 Bake 20 minutes or until toothpick inserted in center comes out clean.

4 Meanwhile, beat remaining 1/4 cup cocoa, remaining 1/2 cup butter, milk, powdered sugar and remaining 1 teaspoon vanilla until smooth.

5 Pour sugar mixture over warm cake. Sprinkle with nuts or coconut, if desired. Cool cake in pan on wire rack.

20 servings

LEMON POPPY SEED CAKE

BETTY BARRETT
OAKHURST, CALIFORNIA

1 1/4 cups all-purpose flour

2/3 cup sugar

1/2 cup cornstarch

1 tablespoon poppy seeds

2 1/4 teaspoons baking powder

1 teaspoon salt

2 tablespoons butter

1 cup skim milk

2 teaspoons freshly grated lemon peel

1 1/2 teaspoons vanilla

1 egg

1 Heat oven to 350°F. Spray 8-inch round cake pan with nonstick cooking spray; lightly flour.

2 In large bowl, whisk together flour, sugar, cornstarch, poppy seeds, baking powder and salt. Blend in butter with fingers until incorporated.

3 In large measuring cup or bowl, lightly beat together milk, lemon peel, vanilla and egg. Stir milk mixture into flour mixture until just blended. Pour batter into pan.

4 Bake 35 minutes or until toothpick inserted in center comes out clean. Cool in pan 10 minutes on wire rack. Remove from pan; cool completely.

8 servings

WACKY CAKE WITH CARAMEL ICING

WACKY CAKE WITH CARAMEL ICING

LEEANN WHEELER
GRANTS, NEW MEXICO

CAKE

3 cups all-purpose flour

2 cups sugar

2 cups cold water

1½ cups oil

6 tablespoons unsweetened cocoa*

1 teaspoon salt

2 tablespoons apple cider vinegar

2 teaspoons vanilla

2 teaspoons soda water

ICING

2 tablespoons butter

½ cup packed brown sugar

3 tablespoons milk

¾ cup sugar

1 Heat oven to 350°F. Spray 13x9-inch pan with nonstick cooking spray.

2 In large bowl, combine flour, sugar, water, oil, cocoa, salt, vinegar, vanilla and soda water; mix thoroughly. Pour into pan.

3 Bake 30 to 40 minutes or until toothpick inserted in center comes out clean. Cool in pan on wire rack.

4 To prepare icing, melt butter in small saucepan over medium heat. Stir in brown sugar. Cook, stirring constantly, until sugar melts and mixture is bubbly. Remove from heat. Cool 5 minutes. Stir in milk. Beat in sugar at low speed 1 minute. Beat at medium speed another minute or until frosting is smooth. Spread over cake.

TIP *For an easy and delicious white cake, omit unsweetened cocoa.

16 servings

CHOCOLATE-ZUCCHINI CAKE

CHRIS McBEE
XENIA, OHIO

2 cups all-purpose flour

1 teaspoon baking powder

1 teaspoon baking soda

½ teaspoon salt

1 teaspoon cinnamon

¼ cup unsweetened cocoa

3 eggs

1½ cups sugar

½ cup vegetable oil

¾ cup buttermilk

2 medium zucchini, coarsely shredded

1 teaspoon vanilla

1 cup coarsely chopped walnuts

½ cup raisins

1 tablespoon powdered sugar

1 Heat oven to 350°F. Spray 10-cup Bundt pan with nonstick cooking spray.

2 In large bowl, combine flour, baking powder, baking soda, salt, cinnamon and cocoa; mix well. Set aside.

3 In another large bowl, beat eggs at high speed until light and fluffy. Gradually beat in sugar. In medium bowl, stir together vegetable oil, buttermilk and zucchini. Gradually add and stir in zucchini mixture alternately with dry ingredients. Stir in vanilla, walnuts and raisins at low speed. Pour into pan.

4 Bake 55 to 60 minutes or until toothpick inserted in center comes out clean. Cool in pan on wire rack 10 minutes; invert cake and cool completely. Just before serving, sift powdered sugar over cake.

12 servings

MELT-IN-YOUR-MOUTH BLUEBERRY CAKE

STEPHANIE WICKE
VALPARAISO, INDIANA

2 eggs, separated

1 cup sugar plus 2 tablespoons

$1/2$ cup butter

$1/2$ teaspoon salt

1 teaspoon vanilla

$1^1/2$ cups all-purpose flour

1 teaspoon baking powder

$1/3$ cup milk

$1^1/2$ cups blueberries, dusted with flour

1 teaspoon cinnamon

1 Heat oven to 350°F. Spray 8-inch square pan with nonstick cooking spray.

2 In large bowl, beat egg whites at medium speed until foamy; beat in $1/4$ cup of the sugar. Continue beating until stiff peaks form.

3 In another large bowl, beat butter, salt, vanilla, $3/4$ cup sugar and egg yolks until light and creamy.

4 In another bowl, sift together flour and baking powder. Stir gradually into batter, alternating with milk. Fold in egg whites and blueberries. Spoon into pan. Combine remaining 2 tablespoons sugar and cinnamon; sprinkle over batter.

5 Bake 50 minutes or until toothpick inserted in center comes out clean. Cool cake in pan on wire rack.

9 servings

APPLESAUCE SPICE CAKE WITH PENUCHE FROSTING

RHONDA HARRELL
CHINO HILLS, CALIFORNIA

CAKE

$1/2$ cup shortening

$2^1/2$ cups all-purpose flour

2 cups sugar

$3/4$ teaspoon salt

$3/4$ teaspoon baking soda

$1/4$ teaspoon baking powder

1 teaspoon cinnamon

$1/2$ teaspoon allspice

$1/2$ teaspoon ground cloves

$3/4$ teaspoon nutmeg

$1/2$ cup milk

2 eggs

2 cups applesauce

FROSTING

$1/2$ cup butter

1 cup packed brown sugar

1 teaspoon vanilla

$1/4$ cup milk

3 cups powdered sugar

1 Heat oven to 350°F. Spray 13x9-inch pan with nonstick cooking spray.

2 In large bowl, beat together shortening and flour at medium speed. In medium bowl, mix together sugar, salt, baking soda, baking powder, cinnamon, allspice, cloves and nutmeg. Stir into shortening mixture gradually. Add $1/2$ cup milk, eggs and applesauce; mix thoroughly at medium speed. Pour into pan.

3 Bake 45 to 50 minutes or until toothpick inserted in center comes out clean. Cool cake in pan on wire rack.

4 To prepare frosting, melt butter in small saucepan over medium heat; stir in brown sugar. Cook until bubbly. Add vanilla, stir and remove from heat. Add $1/4$ cup milk; beat vigorously by hand until smooth. Beat in enough powdered sugar for smooth frosting. Frost cake quickly.

12 servings

JUNIE'S PINEAPPLE CAKE

PEGGY WINKWORTH
DURANGO, COLORADO

CAKE

2 cups sugar

2 cups all-purpose flour

2 teaspoons baking soda

2 eggs, slightly beaten

1 (20-oz.) can crushed pineapple with juice

1 cup chopped walnuts

FROSTING

1 (8-oz.) pkg. cream cheese, softened

$1/2$ cup butter, softened

2 cups powdered sugar

1 teaspoon vanilla

1 Heat oven to 350°F. Spray 13x9-inch pan with nonstick cooking spray.

2 In large bowl, stir together sugar, flour, baking soda, eggs, pineapple and $3/4$ cup of the walnuts. Pour mixture into pan.

3 Bake 30 to 45 minutes or until toothpick inserted in center comes out clean. Cool cake in pan on wire rack.

4 To prepare frosting, beat cream cheese, butter, powdered sugar and vanilla at medium speed in large bowl until frosting is smooth. Frost cake while slightly warm. Sprinkle with remaining $1/4$ cup walnuts. Store in refrigerator.

16 servings

COCONUT BREAD

DOROTHY H. JOHNSON
HECTOR, MINNESOTA

BREAD

4 eggs

2 cups sugar

1 cup vegetable oil

2 teaspoons coconut extract

3 cups all-purpose flour

$1/2$ teaspoon baking powder

$1/2$ teaspoon baking soda

1 cup buttermilk

1 cup coconut

1 cup nuts, if desired

GLAZE

$1 1/2$ cups sugar

3 tablespoons butter

$3/4$ cup water

1 teaspoon coconut extract

1 Heat oven to 325°F. Spray 2 (9x5-inch) loaf pans with nonstick cooking spray, lightly flour.

2 In large bowl, combine eggs, 2 cups sugar, oil and 2 teaspoons coconut extract. Gradually add and stir in flour, baking powder and baking soda alternately with buttermilk. Stir in coconut and nuts. Pour mixture into pans.

3 Bake 1 hour or until toothpick inserted in center comes out clean. Cool slightly in pans on wire rack; remove from pans.

4 To prepare glaze, combine $1 1/2$ cups sugar, butter, water and 1 teaspoon coconut extract in medium saucepan. Heat to boiling; cook 5 minutes, stirring occasionally. Pour over warm breads. Let stand 3 to 4 hours. Store in refrigerator.

2 loaves

OLD-FASHIONED APPLESAUCE CAKE

STEPHANIE BAKER
HAMDEN, OHIO

1/2 cup butter

2 cups sugar

3 eggs

3 cups all-purpose flour

2 teaspoons baking soda

1 teaspoon salt

2 tablespoons cinnamon

1/2 teaspoon ground nutmeg

1/2 teaspoon allspice

2 cups applesauce

1 cup raisins

3/4 cup chopped walnuts

1 Heat oven to 350°F. Spray 13x9-inch pan with nonstick cooking spray.

2 In large bowl, beat butter, sugar and eggs at medium-high speed until light and fluffy. In another large bowl, sift together flour, baking soda, salt, cinnamon, nutmeg and allspice. Stir flour mixture gradually in butter mixture, alternating with applesauce. Stir in raisins and nuts. Pour into pan.

3 Bake 50 to 60 minutes or until toothpick inserted in center comes out clean. Cool in pan on wire rack. Sprinkle with powdered sugar or top with cream cheese icing, if desired.

12 servings

BLUEBERRY TEA CAKE WITH LEMON SAUCE

KIM KOPPLIN
GRAND JUNCTION, COLORADO

CAKE

2 cups all-purpose flour

1 cup sugar

2 teaspoons baking powder

1/4 teaspoon salt

1/3 cup shortening

3/4 cup milk

1 egg

1 cup rinsed fresh blueberries

SAUCE

1/4 cup sugar

1 teaspoon cornstarch

3 teaspoons lemon juice

1 cup water

1 teaspoon grated lemon peel

1 teaspoon butter

1 Heat oven to 350°F. Spray 8-inch square pan with nonstick cooking spray.

2 In large bowl, combine flour, 1 cup sugar, baking powder and 1/4 teaspoon salt; mix in shortening. Add milk; beat vigorously by hand 2 minutes. Add egg and beat an additional 1 minute. Carefully fold in blueberries. Pour into pan.

3 Bake 50 minutes or until toothpick inserted in center comes out clean. Cool 30 minutes in pan on wire rack.

4 To prepare sauce, stir together 1/4 cup sugar, cornstarch, lemon juice and water in medium saucepan. Stir until smooth. Add lemon peel. Cook over medium heat until mixture thickens and becomes clear, stirring frequently. Remove from heat. Add butter; stir until butter is melted and well incorporated. Spread over cake.

9 servings

BLUEBERRY TEA CAKE
WITH LEMON SAUCE

COMPANY CRANBERRY TEA CAKE

GWEN CAMPBELL
STERLING, VIRGINIA

1 cup fresh cranberries, halved

¾ cup sugar

1 egg

2 cups all-purpose flour

2 teaspoons baking powder

1 teaspoon ground allspice

¼ teaspoon salt

⅓ cup milk

3 tablespoons butter, softened

1 teaspoon vanilla

¾ cup toasted almonds, coursely chopped

1 Heat oven to 350°F. Spray 11x7-inch pan with nonstick cooking spray.

2 In large bowl, combine cranberries with 2 tablespoons of the sugar; set aside. In medium bowl, beat egg; gradually beat in ½ cup sugar.

3 Sift together flour, baking powder, allspice and salt. Add to egg mixture alternately with milk, mixing well. Add butter and vanilla; beat thoroughly. Fold in cranberries and almonds. Pour mixture into pan; sprinkle with remaining 2 tablespoons sugar.

4 Bake 30 minutes or until toothpick inserted in center comes out clean. Cool in pan on wire rack. Serve warm or at room temperature.

12 servings

FRESH APPLE CAKE

ARTIS OLSON
GRANITE FALLS, MINNESOTA

CAKE

¼ cup butter

1 cup sugar

1 egg

1 cup all-purpose flour

1 teaspoon baking soda

½ teaspoon cinnamon

½ teaspoon salt

2 cups chopped apples

½ cup chopped walnuts

SAUCE

¼ cup butter

¼ cup half-and-half

¼ cup sugar

¼ cup packed brown sugar

1 teaspoon all-purpose flour

1 teaspoon vanilla

1 Heat oven to 350°F. Spray 9-inch round cake pan with nonstick cooking spray.

2 Beat ¼ cup butter and 1 cup sugar at medium speed until light and fluffy. Add egg; mix well. Stir together 1 cup flour, baking soda, cinnamon and salt; add to butter mixture. Fold in apples; spoon into prepared pan. Sprinkle walnuts on top of mixture.

3 Bake 40 to 45 minutes or until toothpick inserted into center comes out clean. Cool in pan on wire rack.

4 To prepare sauce, heat ¼ cup butter, half-and-half, ¼ cup sugar, brown sugar and 1 teaspoon flour in heavy saucepan. Bring to a boil; cook until sugars are dissolved. Add vanilla. Spread on cake.

9 servings

SAUCEPAN RAISIN SPICE CAKE WITH CARAMEL FROSTING

LENA RICE
BOISE, IDAHO

CAKE

1 cup raisins

2 cups water

$\frac{1}{2}$ cup shortening

1 cup sugar

$1\frac{3}{4}$ cups all-purpose flour

1 teaspoon baking soda

1 teaspoon cinnamon

1 teaspoon ground cloves

1 teaspoon ground nutmeg

$\frac{1}{2}$ cup chopped nuts

FROSTING

$\frac{1}{4}$ cup butter

$\frac{1}{2}$ cup packed brown sugar

3 tablespoons milk

$\frac{1}{2}$ teaspoon vanilla

2 cups powdered sugar

1 Heat oven to 350°F. Spray 3-quart casserole with nonstick cooking spray.

2 In large saucepan, simmer raisins in water 10 minutes; remove from heat. While still warm, add shortening and sugar. Cool 5 minutes. Add flour, baking soda, cinnamon, cloves, nutmeg and nuts; mix well. Pour into baking dish.

3 Bake 35 to 40 minutes or until toothpick inserted in center comes out clean. Cool in pan on wire rack.

4 To prepare frosting, melt butter in medium saucepan over low heat. Add brown sugar; cook until blended and hot. Add milk; bring to a boil. Boil 30 seconds. Remove from heat; beat in vanilla and enough powdered sugar for a smooth frosting.

12 servings

AUNT GRACE'S BANANA BREAD

CARLENE S. GOODEILL
CHICO, CALIFORNIA

$\frac{3}{4}$ cup butter

$1\frac{1}{2}$ cups sugar

$1\frac{1}{2}$ cups mashed bananas

2 eggs, beaten

1 teaspoon vanilla

2 cups all-purpose flour

1 teaspoon baking soda

$\frac{3}{4}$ teaspoon salt

$\frac{2}{3}$ cup buttermilk*

$\frac{3}{4}$ cup walnuts, chopped

1 Heat oven to 325°F. Spray 2 ($8\frac{1}{2}$ x$4\frac{1}{2}$ x$2\frac{1}{2}$-inch) loaf pans with nonstick cooking spray.

2 In large bowl, beat butter and sugar at medium speed until smooth. Stir in bananas, eggs and vanilla. In another bowl, mix together flour, baking soda and salt; stir into banana mixture alternately with buttermilk. Fold in nuts.

3 Bake 1 hour and 15 minutes or until toothpick inserted in center comes out clean. Cool in pans on wire rack. Remove from pans. Store in refrigerator.

TIP *To substitute for buttermilk, use 2 teaspoons lemon juice plus regular milk to make $\frac{2}{3}$ cup.

2 loaves

BUTTERSCOTCH PECANNANA BREAD
ZUCCHINI-PISTACHIO BREAD

BUTTERSCOTCH PECANNANA BREAD

GWEN CAMPBELL
STERLING, VIRGINIA

3 1/2 cups all-purpose flour

4 teaspoons baking powder

1 teaspoon baking soda

1 teaspoon cinnamon

1 teaspoon nutmeg

1/4 teaspoon mace

1 teaspoon salt

2 1/4 cups mashed ripe bananas

1 1/2 cups packed brown sugar

2 eggs

1/2 cup melted butter

1/2 cup milk

3 cups chopped pecans

2 cups butterscotch or semisweet chocolate chips (12 oz.)

1 Heat oven to 350°F. Spray 2 (9x5-inch) loaf pans with nonstick cooking spray.

2 In large bowl, combine flour, baking powder, baking soda, cinnamon, nutmeg, mace and salt; set aside. In another bowl, combine bananas, brown sugar, eggs and butter; beat at medium speed until smooth. Gradually add flour mixture alternately with milk to banana mixture; blend well. Stir in 2 cups of the pecans and butterscotch chips. Pour mixture into pans; sprinkle with remaining 1 cup pecans.

3 Bake 60 to 70 minutes or until toothpick inserted in center comes out clean. Cool in pans on wire rack; remove from pans. Store in refrigerator.

2 loaves

ZUCCHINI-PISTACHIO BREAD

CHERYL PETERSON

BREAD

1 1/2 cups all-purpose flour

1 1/2 teaspoons baking soda

1/4 teaspoon cinnamon

3/4 cup sugar

2 eggs

1/2 cup vegetable oil

1 teaspoon vanilla

1/2 teaspoon salt

1 1/2 cups grated zucchini, squeezed dry

1 1/2 cups toasted shelled pistachios, coarsely chopped

FROSTING

1 pasteurized egg white

3/4 cup sugar

2 1/2 tablespoons cold water

1/8 teaspoon cream of tartar

3/4 teaspoon light corn syrup

1/2 teaspoon vanilla

1 Heat oven to 350°F. Spray 9x5-inch loaf pan with nonstick cooking spray.

2 In large bowl, mix together flour, baking soda and cinnamon. In another bowl, whisk together 3/4 cup sugar, eggs, oil, 1 teaspoon vanilla and salt. Add to flour mixture; stir until combined. Fold in zucchini and nuts. Spoon batter into pan.

3 Bake 50 to 60 minutes or until toothpick inserted into center comes out clean. Cool in pan on wire rack. Remove from pan.

4 To prepare frosting, combine egg white, 3/4 cup sugar, water, cream of tartar and corn syrup in double boiler over simmering water. Using hand mixer, beat mixture 7 minutes or until thick and fluffy. Beat in 1/2 teaspoon vanilla. Spread over loaf. Store in refrigerator.

1 loaf

HAWAIIAN REGENT MANGO BREAD

DOLORES NELSON
ROSEBURG, OREGON

1 cup vegetable oil

3/4 cup sugar

3 eggs

2 cups all-purpose flour

2 teaspoons baking powder

1/2 teaspoon cinnamon

1/2 teaspoon ground nutmeg

2 cups chopped fresh mango

1/4 cup macadamia nuts

1/4 cup chopped dates

1/4 cup raisins

1 Heat oven to 350°F. Spray 1(8$\frac{1}{2}$ x4$\frac{1}{2}$ x2$\frac{1}{2}$-inch) loaf pan with nonstick cooking spray.

2 In large bowl, beat oil, sugar and eggs at medium speed until smooth. Stir in flour, baking powder, cinnamon and nutmeg just until moistened. Stir in mango, nuts, dates and raisins. Pour into pan.

3 Bake 1 hour or until toothpick inserted in center comes out clean. Cool in pan on wire rack. Remove from pan. Store in refrigerator.

1 loaf

PAM'S GRAND PRIZE-WINNING ZUCCHINI-BUTTERSCOTCH NUT BREAD

PAM MILLIGAN
ARROYO GRANDE, CALIFORNIA

3 ripe bananas, mashed

2 cups packed brown sugar

3$\frac{1}{2}$ cups all-purpose flour

2 teaspoons baking soda

1/2 teaspoon baking powder

1 teaspoon salt

3 eggs

1 cup vegetable oil

1 tablespoon vanilla

1 (15-oz.) can cream of coconut*

2 cups grated zucchini

1$\frac{1}{2}$ cups chopped walnuts

1 cup butterscotch chips (6 oz.)

1 Heat oven to 350°F. Spray 2 (8$\frac{1}{2}$ x4$\frac{1}{2}$ x2$\frac{1}{2}$-inch) loaf pans with nonstick cooking spray.

2 In large bowl, beat bananas and brown sugar at low speed until combined. In separate bowl, combine flour, baking soda, baking powder and salt.

3 In another large bowl, beat eggs at medium speed. Beat in oil, vanilla, cream of coconut and banana mixture. Add flour mixture, zucchini, walnuts and butterscotch chips; beat well. Spoon mixture into pans.

4 Bake 45 to 60 minutes or until toothpick inserted in center comes out clean. Cool slightly in pans on wire racks; remove from pans. Serve warm slices with one scoop vanilla ice cream drizzled with caramel sauce, if desired. Store in refrigerator.

TIP *Cream of coconut can be found in liquor stores.

2 loaves

CARROT BREAD

JUNE POEPPING
QUINCY, ILLINOIS

BREAD

1 cup vegetable oil

3/4 cup sugar

2 eggs

1 teaspoon vanilla

1 1/2 cups all-purpose flour

1 1/2 teaspoons baking soda

1 1/2 teaspoons cinnamon

1/2 teaspoon salt

1 1/2 cups shredded carrots

1 1/2 cups chopped nuts

GLAZE

1/2 cup powdered sugar

1 teaspoon grated lemon peel

1 tablespoon lemon juice

1 Heat oven to 350°F. Spray 9x5-inch loaf pan with nonstick cooking spray.

2 In large bowl, combine oil, sugar, eggs and vanilla. In separate bowl, combine flour, baking soda, cinnamon and salt. Add to oil mixture; mix just until moistened. Stir in carrots and nuts. Pour mixture into pan.

3 Bake 60 to 70 minutes or until toothpick inserted in center comes out clean. Cool in pan on wire rack 10 minutes. Remove from pan; let cool completely.

4 Meanwhile, mix powdered sugar, lemon peel and juice. Drizzle over top of cooled bread. Store in refrigerator.

1 loaf

STRAWBERRY NICE BREAD

HERMAN STAHL
JOHNSON CITY, NEW YORK

1 3/4 cups all-purpose flour

2 teaspoons baking powder

1/4 teaspoon baking soda

1/8 teaspoon salt

2 eggs, beaten

1/2 cup sugar

1/3 cup vegetable oil

1/2 cup mashed fresh strawberries

1/2 cup strawberry preserves

1/4 cup chopped walnuts

1 Heat oven to 350°F. Spray 9x5-inch loaf pan with nonstick cooking spray.

2 In large bowl, mix together flour, baking powder, baking soda and salt. In another bowl, combine eggs, sugar and oil. Add to flour mixture; mix well. Stir in strawberries, preserves and walnuts. Spoon mixture into pan.

3 Bake 50 minutes or until toothpick inserted in center comes out clean. Cool in pan on wire rack. Remove from pan. Store in refrigerator.

1 loaf

PIES, CRISPS &

FRUIT COBBLERS

AUTUMN CARAMEL APPLE PIE (page 40)

SOUR CREAM PIE SHELL

CHARLOTTE WARD
HILTON HEAD, SOUTH CAROLINA

¼ cup plus 2 tablespoons sour cream

2 tablespoons ice water

1 teaspoon sugar

¾ teaspoon salt

2½ cups all-purpose flour

½ cup butter, chilled, cut up

½ cup shortening, chilled

1 In small bowl, combine sour cream, ice water, sugar and salt. In large bowl, combine flour, butter and shortening with fingers or pastry blender until mixture crumbles. Add sour cream mixture; stir together just until dough forms.

2 Turn dough out onto lightly floured surface; divide in half. Form each half into ball; flatten into 6-inch disk. Wrap each disk in resealable plastic bag; refrigerate 1 hour.

3 Roll crust ⅛ inch thick; press into 2 (9-inch) pie pans. Refrigerate 30 minutes before adding filling of your choice. If baking without filling, refrigerate 45 minutes to 1 hour. Store in refrigerator.

2 (9-inch) pie shells

PINA COLADA PIE

BRISBIN FAMILY
BAY CITY, MICHIGAN

CRUST

2 cups crushed graham crackers

½ cup coconut, toasted

½ cup melted butter

FILLING

¼ cup cornstarch

⅔ cup sugar

¼ teaspoon salt

3 cups cream

3 egg yolks, slightly beaten

½ teaspoon vanilla

2 tablespoons butter

1 cup shredded coconut

½ cup crushed pineapple, well drained

TOPPING

3 egg whites

¼ teaspoon cream of tartar

6 tablespoons sugar

¼ cup toasted coconut

Maraschino cherries

1 Heat oven to 400°F.

2 In 9-inch pie pan, combine crackers, ½ cup coconut and ½ cup butter. Press firmly and evenly against sides and bottom. Refrigerate 1 hour or until firm.

3 To prepare filling, combine cornstarch, ⅔ cup sugar and salt in medium saucepan. Slowly whisk in cream. Bring to a boil over medium heat, stirring constantly. In small bowl, add ½ cup hot cream mixture to egg yolks. Whisk together; pour back into saucepan. Cook 5 minutes, stirring constantly, until thickened. Remove from heat.

4 Add vanilla, 2 tablespoons butter, 1 cup coconut and pineapple; mix well. Cool slightly; pour into crust. Refrigerate.

5 To prepare topping, combine egg whites and cream of tartar in large bowl. Beat at medium speed until frothy. Increase speed to medium-high. Add 6 tablespoons sugar, 1 tablespoon at a time, until sugar is dissolved and stiff peaks form. Spread topping over pie; form peaks with back of spoon. Top with ¼ cup toasted coconut. Bake 8 minutes or until top is slightly browned. Refrigerate at least 3 hours. Garnish with cherries. Store in refrigerator.

10 servings

MOM'S CHERRY CRUNCH DESSERT

PEGGY WINKWORTH
DURANGO, COLORADO

1 1/2 cups all-purpose flour

3/4 cup old-fashioned or quick-cooking oats

1 cup packed brown sugar

1/2 teaspoon baking soda

1/2 teaspoon salt

1/2 cup butter, softened

1 (22-oz.) can cherry pie filling

1 Heat oven to 350°F.

2 In medium bowl, combine flour, oats, brown sugar, baking soda and salt. Cut in butter using two knives or pastry blender until mixture crumbles.

3 Press one-half of mixture into ungreased 9-inch square pan. Pour pie filling into pie shell; sprinkle remaining crumbly mixture over pie filling.

4 Bake 40 to 50 minutes or until lightly browned. Cool on wire rack.

8 servings

UPSIDE-DOWN CARAMEL APPLE PIE

CLAUDIA WENDEL
FRESNO, CALIFORNIA

3 tablespoons butter, softened

1 (15-oz.) pkg. refrigerated pie crusts

1 1/2 cups pecan halves

1/2 cup packed brown sugar

1 cup sugar

2 tablespoons all-purpose flour

1/4 teaspoon salt

1/2 teaspoon cinnamon

1/4 teaspoon nutmeg

1/8 teaspoon allspice

5 cups peeled sliced apples

1 Heat oven to 450°F. Line 9-inch pie pan with 14-inch circle of aluminum foil. Spread 2 tablespoons of the butter over bottom and sides of aluminum foil.

2 Press pecan halves into butter around sides and bottom of pan. Sprinkle with brown sugar. Spray edges of pan with nonstick cooking spray.

3 Place one pie crust over pecans; press evenly. In large bowl, stir together sugar, flour, salt, cinnamon, nutmeg and allspice. Toss apples in flour mixture; spoon into pastry in plate. Dot with remaining 1 tablespoon butter. Cover with second pie crust; crimp edges. Cut two or three slits in top crust.

4 Bake 10 minutes. Reduce oven temperature to 375°F. Bake an additional 35 to 40 minutes or until pastry is golden brown. Remove from oven and cool 5 minutes. Invert onto serving plate. Serve warm.

8 servings

DELUXE CHOCOLATE CREAM
PIE WITH MERINGUE

DELUXE CHOCOLATE CREAM PIE WITH MERINGUE

MRS. FAYNELL BEAVER
LANDIS, NORTH CAROLINA

2 (1-oz.) squares unsweetened chocolate

1 cup plus 6 tablespoons sugar

1/4 teaspoon salt

3 tablespoons cornstarch

3 eggs, separated

2 1/2 cups milk, warm

2 tablespoons butter

1/2 teaspoon vanilla

1 (9-inch) baked pie shell

1 Heat oven to 350°F.

2 In medium saucepan, melt chocolate over low heat. In small bowl, combine 1 cup of the sugar, salt and cornstarch; stir into chocolate. Stir in egg yolks and milk. Cook over medium heat until thickened, stirring constantly. Remove from heat; stir in butter and vanilla. Pour into pie shell; set aside.

3 To prepare meringue, beat egg whites at medium speed until foamy. Beat in remaining 6 tablespoons of the sugar, 1 tablespoon at a time; continue to beat until stiff and glossy. Spread meringue over pie, making sure meringue is touching crust around entire edge. Bake 12 to 15 minutes or until meringue is lightly browned. Cool on wire rack. Store in refrigerator.

8 servings

PECAN PIE IN SPICY PECAN CRUST

AMY SMOUSE
CORTEZ, COLORADO

FILLING

3 eggs

1 cup corn syrup

1/2 cup packed brown sugar

1/4 cup sugar

1/3 cup melted butter

1 tablespoon brandy

1/2 teaspoon vanilla

1 1/2 cups pecan halves

CRUST

1 cup all-purpose flour

1/4 cup ground pecans

1 teaspoon cinnamon

1 teaspoon nutmeg

1/4 teaspoon salt

1/3 cup shortening

1/2 teaspoon brandy

2 to 4 tablespoons cold water

1 Heat oven to 350°F.

2 For filling, beat eggs at medium speed in large bowl. Stir in corn syrup, brown sugar, sugar, butter, 1 tablespoon brandy and vanilla. Stir in 1 1/2 cups pecans. Set aside.

3 For crust, stir together flour, 1/4 cup pecans, cinnamon, nutmeg and salt in medium bowl. Cut in shortening with two knives or pastry blender until mixture crumbles. Sprinkle 1/2 teaspoon brandy over mixture; blend with fork. Sprinkle in water, 1 teaspoon at a time, just until dough forms a ball. Refrigerate 15 minutes.

4 On floured surface, roll dough into 12-inch circle; press into 9-inch pie pan. Flute edges. Pour filling into crust; cover edges with aluminum foil and bake 25 minutes. Remove aluminum foil and bake an additional 30 minutes or until lightly browned. Cool on wire rack. Store in refrigerator.

8 servings

COUNTRY RHUBARB PIE

FANNIE LINE
MILLERSBURG, OHIO

FILLING

1 egg

1 teaspoon vanilla

1 cup sugar

1 tablespoon all-purpose flour

$1/2$ teaspoon cinnamon

$1/4$ teaspoon freshly grated nutmeg

3 cups sliced ($1/2$-inch thick) rhubarb

1 (9-inch) unbaked pie shell

TOPPING

$1/2$ cup butter, softened

$1/2$ cup all-purpose flour

$1/4$ cup packed brown sugar

$1/4$ cup sugar

$1/4$ cup chopped walnuts

2 tablespoons old-fashioned or quick-cooking oats

1 Heat oven to 400°F.

2 In large bowl, beat eggs slightly; add vanilla. In another bowl, stir together 1 cup sugar, 1 tablespoon flour, cinnamon and nutmeg; add to egg mixture. Add rhubarb; pour into pie shell. Stir together butter, $1/2$ cup flour, brown sugar, $1/4$ cup sugar, walnuts and oats until crumbly; sprinkle over rhubarb.

3 Bake 10 minutes. Reduce oven temperature to 350°F; bake an additional 40 minutes or until crust is golden brown. Cool on wire rack. Store in refrigerator.

8 servings

WILMA SHORTCAKE

KAY SPARKMAN
ALEXANDRIA, VIRGINIA

3 cups all-purpose flour

$4^1/2$ teaspoons baking powder

$1^1/2$ teaspoons salt

5 tablespoons sugar

$3/4$ cup butter

2 eggs, slightly beaten

$1/2$ cup milk

1 Heat oven to 400°F.

2 In large bowl, whisk together flour, baking powder, salt and sugar. Cut in butter using two knives or pastry blender until mixture crumbles. Add eggs and milk; mix thoroughly.

3 Shape dough into individual cakes about 3 inches in diameter; place in 13x9-inch pan. Bake 15 minutes or until golden brown. Serve warm with sliced fruit and whipped cream or ice cream, if desired.

12 servings

BLACKBERRY COBBLER

TAMMY RAYNES
NATCHITOCHES, LOUISIANA

$1/2$ cup melted butter

1 cup all-purpose flour

$1^1/2$ teaspoons baking powder

$1/8$ teaspoon salt

1 cup sugar

$3/4$ cup milk

1 teaspoon vanilla

4 cups fresh blackberries or 2 (10-oz.) pkg. frozen blackberries, thawed

1 Heat oven to 375°F.

2 Pour butter into 2-quart casserole; set aside. In large bowl, combine flour, baking powder, salt and sugar; stir well. Add milk, vanilla and blackberries to flour mixture; stir until well blended. Spoon batter into casserole (do not stir).

3 Bake, uncovered, 40 to 45 minutes or until golden brown. Serve warm. Store in refrigerator.

6 servings

PEACH PIE

THERESA GAUDETTE
NORTH NEW PORTLAND, MAINE

2 (9-inch) unbaked pie shells

3 cups sliced fresh peaches

1 cup sugar

3 tablespoons all-purpose flour

3 tablespoons butter

1/4 teaspoon nutmeg

1/4 teaspoon cinnamon

1 Heat oven to 400°F.

2 Place 1 pie shell in 9-inch pie pan. In medium bowl, combine peaches, sugar, flour, 2 tablespoons of the butter, nutmeg and cinnamon; pour into crust. Dot with remaining 1 tablespoon butter. Top with remaining pastry; crimp edges.

3 Bake 45 to 50 minutes or until crust is golden brown. Cool on wire rack. Serve warm or cool with ice cream or whipped cream, if desired.

8 servings

CHESS PIES

SANDRA K. SNETHEN
MINNEAPOLIS, MINNESOTA

1/2 cup butter

1 cup sugar

2 eggs

1 cup raisins or chopped dates

1 cup finely chopped walnuts

1 teaspoon vanilla

1 (15-oz.) pkg. refrigerated pie crusts

1 Heat oven to 350°F.

2 In large bowl, beat together butter and sugar at high speed until fluffy. Beat in eggs. Stir in raisins, walnuts and vanilla.

3 Unfold pie crusts. Using 3 1/2-inch round cutter, cut 12 circles from pie crust rounds. Place pie crust circles in each of 12 regular-size muffin cups, pressing into bottoms and up sides of cups. Divide filling evenly among cups.

4 Bake 25 to 30 minutes or until set. Cool on wire rack. Store in refrigerator.

12 servings

JEN'S CRUMBLY APPLE PIE

JENNIFER GULLO
RENO, NEVADA

CRUST

1 cup all-purpose flour

1/2 teaspoon salt

1/3 cup shortening, chilled

1/4 cup ice water

FILLING

7 Granny Smith apples, peeled, cored, very thinly sliced

1/2 cup sugar

1 teaspoon cinnamon

1/4 teaspoon nutmeg

1/4 teaspoon salt

TOPPING

3/4 cup packed brown sugar

3/4 cup all-purpose flour

1/2 teaspoon nutmeg

1/3 cup butter, chilled, cut into small pieces

1 Place oven rack in lowest position. Heat oven to 400°F.

2 To prepare crust, stir together 1 cup flour and 1/2 teaspoon salt in medium bowl. Using 2 knives or pastry blender, cut shortening into flour mixture until mixture crumbles. Add ice water, 1 teaspoon at a time, tossing with fork, until dough forms. Shape into 8-inch disk; wrap in plastic wrap. Refrigerate 30 minutes.

3 On floured work surface, using floured rolling pin, roll dough into 12-inch circle. Press into 9-inch pie pan. Trim excess dough, leaving 1-inch overhang.

4 To prepare filling, combine apple slices, sugar, cinnamon, 1/4 teaspoon nutmeg and 1/4 teaspoon salt in large bowl; mix until well combined. Spoon into crust.

5 To prepare topping, stir together brown sugar, 3/4 cup flour and 1/2 teaspoon nutmeg in small bowl. Cut butter into brown sugar mixture until mixture crumbles. Sprinkle apples evenly over topping. Bake pie about 35 minutes or until topping is lightly browned and filling is bubbly. Cool on wire rack.

8 servings

APPLE CREAM PIE

LIZ BLAKE
BEAUMONT, TEXAS

¾ cup sugar

2 tablespoons all-purpose flour

1 cup sour cream

1 egg, well beaten

½ teaspoon vanilla

⅛ teaspoon salt

2 cups finely chopped tart apples

1 (9-inch) unbaked pie shell

TOPPING

⅓ cup sugar

1 teaspoon cinnamon

⅓ cup all-purpose flour

¼ cup butter, softened

1 Heat oven to 450°F.

2 In large bowl, combine ¾ cup sugar and 2 table-spoons flour; add sour cream, egg, vanilla and salt. Beat at medium speed until smooth. Add apples; mix thoroughly. Pour into pie shell.

3 Bake 15 minutes. Reduce oven temperature to 325°F; bake an additional 30 minutes. In medium bowl, combine ⅓ cup sugar, cinnamon, ⅓ cup flour and butter; sprinkle over pie. Bake an additional 20 minutes or until crust is golden brown. Cool on wire rack. Store in refrigerator.

8 servings

RASPBERRY PIE

THERESA GAUDETTE
NORTH NEW PORTLAND, MAINE

2 (9-inch) baked pie shells

4 cups fresh raspberries

1¼ cups sugar

3 tablespoons cornstarch

1 tablespoon butter

1 Heat oven to 400°F.

2 Line 9-inch pie pan with one of the pie shells. In medium bowl, combine raspberries, sugar and cornstarch. Pour into crust; dot with butter. Top with remaining pie shell.

3 Bake 45 minutes or until crust is golden brown; cool on wire rack.

TIP *For a nice finish to top of pie, brush with beaten egg white and sprinkle with powdered sugar.

16 servings

FRENCH SILK PIE

MARGARET BENHAM
OKLAHOMA CITY, OKLAHOMA

½ cup butter, softened

1½ cups powdered sugar

2 pasteurized eggs

2 (1-oz.) squares unsweetened chocolate, melted

1 teaspoon vanilla

1 (9-inch) baked pie shell

1 In medium bowl, beat butter and powdered sugar at high speed 5 minutes or until fluffy. Add eggs one at a time, beating 1 to 2 minutes after each addition. Add chocolate and vanilla to egg mixture; beat until light and fluffy.

2 Pour mixture into pie shell; refrigerate several hours or overnight. Serve topped with whipped cream and chocolate curls, if desired. Store in refrigerator.

8 servings

RASPBERRY PIE

CHAMPAGNE SWEET POTATO PIE

BRIGITTE LITTLE
EATONTOWN, NEW JERSEY

3 to 4 medium sweet potatoes, peeled, cubed

3 tablespoons butter

1/2 cup sugar

1/2 cup packed brown sugar

1/2 cup Champagne

1/2 cup orange juice

1/4 teaspoon nutmeg

1 teaspoon cinnamon

1/4 teaspoon ground ginger

2 teaspoons vanilla

2 eggs, separated

1/4 to 1/2 cup milk

1 (9-inch) graham-cracker pie shell

1 Heat oven to 350°F. Arrange sweet potatoes in 13x9-inch pan.

2 In medium saucepan, melt butter over low heat. Add sugars; stir until very thick. Add Champagne, orange juice, nutmeg, cinnamon, ginger and vanilla; blend well. Bring to a boil; simmer 2 minutes. Remove from heat; pour mixture over potatoes. Cover and bake 1 hour or until potatoes are very tender.

3 In large bowl, mash potatoes and cooking liquid until smooth. (Or cool potatoes slightly and puree in blender or food processor.) In separate bowl, beat egg whites at medium-high speed until soft peaks form. Beat egg yolks and milk into sweet potato mixture until creamy. Gently fold in egg whites.

4 Pour into pie shell; bake 30 minutes or until set. Garnish with chopped nuts and whipped cream, if desired. Store in refrigerator.

8 servings

FRESH STRAWBERRY GLAZED PIE

SHARON DECKER
CLYMER, PENNSYLVANIA

CRUST

1 1/2 cups graham-cracker crumbs

3 tablespoons sugar

1/3 cup melted butter

FILLING

6 cups small whole fresh strawberries (about 1 1/2 quarts)

1 cup sugar

3 tablespoons cornstarch

1/2 cup water

1 Heat oven to 350°F.

2 In large bowl, combine crumbs and 3 tablespoons sugar; add butter and mix thoroughly. Press mixture into 9-inch pie pan. Bake 10 minutes. Cool completely.

3 Mash 4 cups of the berries. In medium saucepan, stir together 1 cup sugar and cornstarch; gradually stir in water and mashed berries. Cook over medium heat, stirring constantly, until mixture thickens and boils. Boil and stir 1 minute. Cool completely.

4 Fill pie shell with remaining 2 cups berries. Pour glaze over berries; spread to edges of crust carefully to avoid pulling crumbs into glaze. Refrigerate at least 3 hours or until set. Store in refrigerator.

8 servings

JESSIE'S APPLE DUMPLINGS

PEGGY WINKWORTH
DURANGO, COLORADO

1½ cups sugar

1⅛ teaspoons cinnamon

5 tablespoons butter

⅛ teaspoon salt

1 *Sour Cream Pie Shell* (page 26), unbaked

4 apples, peeled, cored

2 cups water

1 Heat oven to 425°F.

2 In small bowl, combine ½ cup of the sugar, ⅛ teaspoon of the cinnamon, 1 tablespoon of the butter and salt; mix until well blended. Divide mixture among apples, placing in center of each apple.

3 Roll out dough on floured surface. Cut square of dough for each apple (dough should be large enough to wrap around apple). Wrap apples with dough. Place dumplings in 13x9-inch aluminum foil-lined pan.

4 In saucepan, combine water, remaining 1 cup sugar, remaining 1 teaspoon cinnamon and remaining 4 tablespoons butter. Simmer 10 minutes. Pour mixture over dumplings. Bake 40 to 45 minutes or until crust is golden and apples are tender. Serve warm or cool. Store in refrigerator.

6 servings

PEACH CRUMBLE

FANNIE KLINE
MILLERSBURG, OHIO

FILLING

5 cups peeled sliced fresh peaches

1 tablespoon lemon juice

1 cup sugar

2 tablespoons all-purpose flour

½ teaspoon nutmeg, freshly grated

TOPPING

2½ cups all-purpose flour

1 cup butter

½ teaspoon salt

½ cup packed brown sugar

½ cup chopped pecans

1 Heat oven to 350°F. Spray 3-quart casserole with nonstick cooking spray.

2 Arrange peaches in bottom of pan; sprinkle with lemon juice. In medium bowl, stir together sugar, 2 tablespoons flour and nutmeg; mix with peaches. Set aside.

3 For topping, combine 2½ cups flour, butter and salt with pastry blender until mixture crumbles. Stir in brown sugar and pecans. Sprinkle over peach mixture.

4 Bake 40 to 50 minutes or until juice bubbles. Cool slightly on wire rack; serve with vanilla ice cream, if desired. Store in refrigerator.

10 servings

GRANDMA BETTY'S UPSIDE-DOWN COBBLER

GRANDMA BETTY'S UPSIDE-DOWN COBBLER

CARLENE GOODEILL
CHICO, CALIFORNIA

¼ cup shortening

½ cup sugar

1 cup all-purpose flour

2 teaspoons baking powder

1 egg

½ cup milk

2 cups fresh berries or sliced fresh peaches

1 Heat oven to 350°F. Spray 8-inch round cake pan with nonstick cooking spray.

2 In medium bowl, combine shortening, sugar, flour, baking powder, egg and milk; mix until well blended. Pour batter into pan. Spoon berries over batter.

3 Bake 45 to 60 minutes or until toothpick inserted in center comes out clean. Cool on wire rack. Store in refrigerator.

6 servings

LEMON-BUTTERMILK PIE

SARAH ROARK
ROSSVILLE, ILLINOIS

4 eggs

¾ cup sugar

2 tablespoons all-purpose flour

1½ cups buttermilk

¼ cup melted butter

1 tablespoon grated lemon peel

3 tablespoons fresh lemon juice

1 teaspoon vanilla

1 (9-inch) unbaked pie shell

½ teaspoon cinnamon

1 Heat oven to 375°F.

2 In large bowl, beat eggs and sugar at medium speed until light and fluffy. Beat in flour, buttermilk, butter, lemon peel, lemon juice and vanilla. Pour into pie shell. Sprinkle with cinnamon.

3 Bake 20 to 30 minutes or until toothpick inserted in center comes out clean. Cool on wire rack. Store in refrigerator.

8 servings

BANANA-CARAMEL PIE

TAMMY RAYNES
NATCHITOCHES, LOUISIANA

¼ cup water

2 egg yolks, beaten

½ cup sugar

½ cup packed brown sugar

¼ cup all-purpose flour

¼ teaspoon salt

1 cup boiling water

1 tablespoon butter

½ teaspoon vanilla

3 to 4 medium bananas, sliced

1 (9-inch) baked pie shell

1 cup heavy cream, whipped

1 In medium saucepan, combine water and egg yolks. Add sugar, brown sugar, flour and salt; stir well. Gradually add boiling water, stirring constantly over medium-low heat 1 to 2 minutes or until mixture is thickened. Remove from heat; add butter and vanilla, stirring until butter melts. Cool 5 minutes, stirring occasionally.

2 Layer banana slices in pie shell; pour filling over bananas. Cover and refrigerate at least 2 hours. Spread whipped cream over pie. Store in refrigerator.

8 servings

YAM PRALINE PIE

LINNIE DAVIS
ELKHART, INDIANA

FILLING

2 eggs

$\frac{1}{2}$ cup sugar

$\frac{1}{2}$ cup packed brown sugar

1 teaspoon cinnamon

$\frac{1}{2}$ teaspoon nutmeg

$\frac{1}{2}$ teaspoon ground ginger

$\frac{1}{4}$ teaspoon salt

2 cups mashed cooked yams

$\frac{3}{4}$ cup milk

1 cup half-and-half

1 (9-inch) unbaked pie shell

TOPPING

$\frac{1}{3}$ cup chopped pecans

$\frac{1}{3}$ cup packed brown sugar

3 tablespoons butter

1 Heat oven to 400°F.

2 In large bowl, beat eggs at medium speed. Add sugar, $\frac{1}{2}$ cup brown sugar, cinnamon, nutmeg, ginger and salt. Stir in yams. Gradually stir in milk and half-and-half. Pour mixture into pie shell.

3 Bake 10 minutes. Reduce oven temperature to 350°F; bake an additional 25 minutes.

4 To prepare topping, combine pecans, $\frac{1}{3}$ cup brown sugar and butter in small bowl; mix until well combined. Sprinkle topping over pie. Bake 20 minutes or until toothpick inserted in center comes out clean. Cool completely on wire rack. Store in refrigerator.

8 servings

AUTUMN CARAMEL APPLE PIE

GWEN CAMPBELL
STERLING, VIRGINIA

4 cups Granny Smith apples, peeled, cored, thinly sliced

2 tablespoons apple juice or water

1 (9-inch) graham-cracker pie shell

$\frac{3}{4}$ cup packed brown sugar

$\frac{3}{4}$ cup graham-cracker crumbs

1 tablespoon all-purpose flour

$\frac{1}{2}$ teaspoon cinnamon

$\frac{1}{2}$ teaspoon nutmeg

$\frac{1}{4}$ teaspoon ground cardamom

$\frac{1}{4}$ cup unsalted melted butter

TOPPING

20 vanilla caramels, unwrapped

3 tablespoons milk

$\frac{1}{4}$ teaspoon rum extract

1 Heat oven to 350°F. In large saucepan, combine apple slices and apple juice; simmer 10 minutes. Pour mixture into large bowl to cool. Pour cooled mixture, including liquid, into pie shell.

2 In another large bowl, combine brown sugar, graham-cracker crumbs, flour, cinnamon, nutmeg, cardamom and butter; sprinkle evenly over apples. Bake 20 minutes or until apples are tender; remove from oven but do not turn oven off.

3 To prepare sauce, combine caramels and milk in medium saucepan over low heat. Stir until melted and smooth; stir in rum extract. Pour hot caramel sauce over pie; return pie to oven. Continue to bake an additional 10 minutes or until caramel just begins to bubble at edge of pie. Cool pie on wire rack.

8 servings

AUTUMN CARAMEL APPLE PIE

GERMAN CHOCOLATE PIE

SHELLY COOPER
MUSKOGEE, OKLAHOMA

1 (4-oz.) bar semisweet chocolate

1/4 cup butter

1 (12-oz.) can unsweetened milk

1 1/2 cups sugar

3 tablespoons cornstarch

1/8 teaspoon salt

2 eggs

1 teaspoon vanilla

2 (9-inch) unbaked pie shells

1 1/3 cups flaked coconut

1/2 cup chopped pecans

1 Heat oven to 375°F.

2 In medium saucepan, melt chocolate and butter over low heat, stirring until chocolate melts. Remove from heat. Gradually stir in milk; set aside.

3 In medium bowl, combine sugar, cornstarch and salt. Add eggs and vanilla; mix well. Gradually stir in chocolate mixture using wire whisk. Pour filling into pie shells; sprinkle with coconut and pecans.

4 Bake 45 minutes or until set. Cool on wire rack. Refrigerate at least 4 hours. Top with whipped cream and chocolate shavings, if desired. Store in refrigerator.

8 servings

COOKIE DREAM PIE

GIGI MORGAN
INDIANAPOLIS, INDIANA

40 chocolate sandwich cookies (about 1-lb.)

1/4 cup melted butter

1/2 cup milk

24 large marshmallows

2 1/2 cups heavy cream, whipped

1 Coarsely chop 10 of the cookies; set aside. Cut 4 cookies in half; set aside. Place remaining 26 cookies in large resealable plastic bag; crush into crumbs using rolling pin.

2 In large bowl, combine crushed cookies and butter; mix well. Press mixture into 9-inch pie pan; refrigerate.

3 To prepare filling, stir milk and marshmallows over medium heat in large saucepan until melted and smooth; cool. Fold 2 cups of the whipped cream into marshmallow mixture. Fold in 10 chopped cookies; pour into chilled crust. Garnish with remaining whipped cream and 4 halved cookies. Refrigerate 4 hours or until firm. Store in refrigerator.

8 servings

NANCY PIE

WENDY KAY TATE
LANCASTER, PENNSYLVANIA

3 egg whites

$\frac{1}{2}$ teaspoon cream of tartar

1$\frac{1}{4}$ cups sugar

1$\frac{1}{2}$ teaspoons vanilla

18 saltine crackers

1 cup chopped pecans

1 cup heavy cream

2 tablespoons unsweetened cocoa

1 Heat oven to 325°F. Spray 9-inch pie pan with cooking spray.

2 In large bowl, combine egg whites and cream of tartar; beat at medium-low speed until egg whites are frothy. Increase speed to medium. Slowly beat in 1 cup of the sugar; add 1 teaspoon of the vanilla.

3 Place crackers in large resealable plastic bag; crush into crumbs using rolling pin. Fold crumbs and pecans into egg white mixture. Spread mixture evenly into pan.

4 Bake 35 minutes; cool to room temperature.

5 In medium bowl, stir together cream, remaining $\frac{1}{4}$ cup of the sugar and cocoa; cover and refrigerate 1 hour. Add remaining $\frac{1}{2}$ teaspoon of the vanilla; whip at medium-high speed until soft peaks form. Spoon dollop of topping onto each serving of pie. Sprinkle with chocolate slivers, if desired. Store in refrigerator.

8 servings

IRISH BANANA DELIGHT PIE

PHYLLIS BUSSE
LEAVENWORTH, WASHINGTON

1 ($\frac{1}{4}$-oz.) pkg. unflavored gelatin

$\frac{1}{4}$ cup cold water

$\frac{3}{4}$ cup sugar

$\frac{1}{4}$ cup cornstarch

$\frac{1}{2}$ teaspoon salt

2$\frac{3}{4}$ cups milk

4 egg yolks, beaten

2 tablespoons butter

1 tablespoon vanilla

4 medium bananas

1 (8-oz.) container frozen whipped topping, thawed

1 teaspoon rum

1 (9-inch) baked pie shell

2 tablespoons fresh lemon juice

2 teaspoons grated lemon peel

1 To prepare custard filling, soften gelatin in cold water; set aside. In medium saucepan, combine sugar, cornstarch and salt. Stir in milk and egg yolks; cook over low heat, stirring constantly, 20 to 25 minutes or until thickened. Remove from heat; stir in softened gelatin until dissolved. Stir in butter and vanilla. Cover surface of custard with plastic wrap; refrigerate 2 hours or until chilled.

2 Slice 3 of the bananas; fold into custard with whipped topping. Stir in rum; spoon into pie shell. Refrigerate 4 to 5 hours or until set. Shortly before serving, place lemon juice in small bowl; slice remaining banana into juice. Drain and pat banana dry. Arrange slices on pie; sprinkle with lemon peel. Serve immediately. Store in refrigerator.

8 servings

CREAM CHEESE PECAN PIE

CREAM CHEESE PECAN PIE

VIVIAN NIKANOW
CHICAGO, ILLINOIS

1 (8-oz.) pkg. cream cheese, softened

$1/3$ cup sugar

4 eggs

2 teaspoons vanilla

1 (9-inch) unbaked pie shell

$1\frac{1}{4}$ cups coarsely chopped pecans

1 cup light corn syrup

$1/4$ teaspoon salt

1 Heat oven to 375°F.

2 In large bowl, beat together cream cheese, sugar, 1 of the eggs and 1 teaspoon of the vanilla at high speed until smooth. Pour mixture into pie shell. Sprinkle pecans over cheese mixture.

3 In small bowl, combine remaining 3 eggs, corn syrup, salt and remaining 1 teaspoon of the vanilla; pour mixture over pecans.

4 Bake 40 minutes or until set. Cool on wire rack. Store in refrigerator.

8 servings

CHOCOLATE MOUSSE PIE

CHRISTINA POOL
SALEM, OREGON

CRUST

$1\frac{2}{3}$ cups all-purpose flour

$1/2$ teaspoon salt

$1/2$ cup shortening

3 to 4 tablespoons cold water

FILLING

$1\frac{1}{2}$ cups miniature marshmallows or 16 large marshmallows

$1/2$ cup milk

1 (8-oz.) bar milk chocolate

1 cup heavy cream

1 Heat oven to 475°F.

2 To prepare crust, combine flour and salt in medium bowl. With pastry blender or two knives, work shortening into flour mixture until mixture crumbles. Sprinkle with water, 1 tablespoon at a time, tossing with fork until flour is moistened and pastry almost cleans side of bowl. Gather pastry into ball; shape into disk on lightly floured cloth-covered surface. Roll pastry to $1/8$ inch thickness with floured cloth-covered rolling pin. Line 9-inch pie pan with dough; press firmly against bottom and sides. Prick bottom and sides thoroughly with fork. Bake 8 to 10 minutes or until light brown; cool.

3 To prepare filling, heat marshmallows, milk and chocolate in medium saucepan over low heat, stirring constantly until melted and mixture is smooth. Refrigerate, stirring occasionally, until mixture mounds slightly when dropped from spoon. Beat cream in chilled bowl at high speed. Fold chocolate mixture into whipped cream. Pour into pie shell. Refrigerate about 8 hours or until set. Spread with whipped cream and garnish with chocolate curls, if desired. Store in refrigerator.

8 servings

NECTARINE-STRAWBERRY COBBLER

NANCY HACKER
EUCLID, OHIO

2 cups peeled sliced nectarines

2 cups sliced strawberries

1 tablespoon lemon juice

1 cup all-purpose flour

1 cup sugar

1/2 teaspoon salt

1 egg, beaten

6 tablespoons melted butter

1 Heat oven to 375°F.

2 Place nectarines and strawberries in bottom of 8-inch square pan. Sprinkle with lemon juice.

3 In large bowl, sift together flour, sugar and salt; add egg, tossing with fork until mixture is crumbly. Sprinkle over fruit; drizzle with melted butter.

4 Bake 35 to 40 minutes or until lightly browned. Cool on wire rack. Serve warm or at room temperature. Store in refrigerator.

8 servings

BRACKLEY TART

MORGANA ABBEY
BUFFALO, NEW YORK

2 cups raisins

1/2 cup honey

2 eggs

1/4 cup chopped crystalized ginger

1/2 teaspoon grated orange or lemon peel

1/4 cup melted butter

1/2 cup packed brown sugar

1 apple, chopped

1/2 teaspoon cinnamon

1/4 teaspoon nutmeg

1/4 teaspoon ground cloves

1 (9-inch) unbaked pie shell

1 Heat oven to 375°F.

2 In large bowl, stir together raisins, honey, eggs, ginger, orange peel, butter, brown sugar, apple, cinnamon, nutmeg and cloves. Pour mixture into pie shell.

3 Bake 40 minutes or until set. Cool on wire rack. Store in refrigerator.

8 servings

PEANUT BUTTER PIE

FRANCES PASSEROTTI
NACOGDOCHES, TEXAS

1 (8-oz.) pkg. cream cheese

1 cup creamy peanut butter

1 cup powdered sugar

1 (8-oz.) container frozen whipped topping, thawed

1 (9-inch) graham-cracker pie shell

1 In large bowl, combine cream cheese and peanut butter; beat at medium speed until creamy. Add powdered sugar; beat until smooth. Fold in one-half of the whipped topping; pour into pie shell.

2 Refrigerate several hours or until firm. Garnish with remaining whipped topping. Store in refrigerator.

8 servings

CHOCOLATE-CHIP PIE

FRANCES PASSEROTTI
NACOGDOCHES, TEXAS

2 eggs, separated

½ cup all-purpose flour

½ cup sugar

½ cup packed brown sugar

1 cup melted butter, cooled

1 cup semisweet chocolate chips (6 oz.)

1 cup chopped walnuts

1 (9-inch) unbaked pie shell

1 Heat oven to 325°F.

2 In large bowl, beat eggs at medium speed until frothy. Add flour, sugar and brown sugar; beat until well blended. Stir in butter, chocolate chips and walnuts. Pour mixture into pie shell.

3 Bake 1 hour or until set. Serve warm with whipped topping or ice cream, if desired. Store in refrigerator.

8 servings

FRESH BLUEBERRY PIE

BOBBI BARBARESE
MOORESTOWN, NEW JERSEY

1 (3 oz.) pkg. cream cheese, softened

1 (9-inch) baked pie shell

5 cups fresh blueberries

½ cup water

½ cup sugar

2 tablespoons cornstarch

2 tablespoons lemon juice

1 Spread cream cheese in bottom of baked pie shell while crust is still warm. Fill with 4 cups of the blueberries.

2 Combine remaining 1 cup blueberries with water in medium saucepan. Bring just to a boil; reduce heat and simmer 2 minutes. Strain and reserve juice; discard berries.

3 Combine sugar and cornstarch in medium saucepan; gradually stir in juice. Cook over medium heat until clear and thick, stirring constantly. Cool slightly; add lemon juice. Pour over berries in pie shell. Refrigerate until set. Store in refrigerator.

8 servings

ANYTIME

COOKIES

SOUR CREAM CUT-OUT COOKIES (page 65)

NO-BAKE FUDGE-OATMEAL COOKIES

JANE M. CHOLMINSKY
PT. PLEASANT, NEW JERSEY

2 cups sugar

$\frac{1}{2}$ cup unsweetened cocoa

$\frac{1}{2}$ cup milk

$\frac{1}{2}$ cup butter

$\frac{1}{2}$ cup peanut butter

1 teaspoon vanilla

3 cups old-fashioned or quick-cooking oats

1 Cover baking sheet with parchment paper. In Dutch oven, combine sugar, cocoa, milk and butter. Bring to a boil. Boil 1 minute; remove from heat. Stir in peanut butter and vanilla. Stir in oats.

2 Drop by spoonfuls onto baking sheets, placing 2 inches apart. Refrigerate 1 hour. Remove from paper.

4 dozen

CANDY-COATED MERINGUE COOKIES

CYNDI GREENE
COTTONDALE, ALABAMA

2 egg whites

$\frac{1}{8}$ teaspoon cream of tartar

$\frac{1}{2}$ cup sugar

$\frac{1}{2}$ cup candy-coated chocolate candies

1 Heat oven to 250°F. Line several baking sheets with parchment paper.

2 In large bowl, beat egg whites and cream of tartar at medium-low speed until frothy. Increase speed to medium; gradually add sugar and beat until glossy stiff peaks form.

3 Fold in candies; drop by teaspoonfuls onto baking sheets, about 2 inches apart. Bake 30 minutes or until firm to the touch, but still white. Cool on baking sheet 5 minutes; transfer to wire rack. Store in airtight container.

2 dozen

CHOCOLATE-ALMOND BISCOTTI

JUNE POEPPING
QUINCY, ILLINOIS

$1\frac{1}{2}$ cups all-purpose flour

$\frac{1}{3}$ cup ground almonds

$\frac{1}{3}$ cup unsweetened cocoa

1 teaspoon baking powder

$\frac{1}{2}$ teaspoon salt

$\frac{1}{2}$ cup butter

$\frac{2}{3}$ cup sugar

2 eggs

1 teaspoon vanilla

$\frac{1}{2}$ teaspoon almond extract

$\frac{1}{2}$ cup slivered almonds

1 Heat oven to 350°F. Line several baking sheets with parchment paper.

2 In medium bowl, mix flour, ground almonds, cocoa, baking powder and salt. Set aside. In large bowl, beat butter and sugar at medium speed until fluffy. Add eggs, vanilla and almond extract; beat until smooth. Add flour mixture; beat until well blended. Gently stir in slivered almonds.

3 On lightly floured board, knead dough into ball; cut in half. Press each piece into 10x4-inch loaf; transfer to baking sheet.

4 Bake about 35 minutes until loaf is set and dry. Cool on baking sheet 10 minutes. Transfer loaf to cutting board.

5 Cut loaf crosswise with sharp knife into $\frac{1}{2}$-inch slices. Return slices to baking sheets, cut-side up. Bake 10 minutes. Cool on wire rack. Store in airtight container.

4 dozen

OATMEAL COOKIES

CATHY LEATHERWOOD
DALLAS, TEXAS

1½ cups all-purpose flour

1 teaspoon salt

1 teaspoon baking soda

1 cup shortening

1 cup packed brown sugar

1 cup sugar

2 eggs, well beaten

1 teaspoon vanilla

3 cups old-fashioned or quick-cooking oats

½ cup chopped nuts

1 In large bowl, combine flour, salt and baking soda; set aside.

2 In another large bowl, beat shortening, brown sugar and sugar at medium speed until well blended and fluffy. Add eggs, vanilla and flour mixture; beat until well blended. Stir in oatmeal and nuts.

3 Shape dough into ¼-inch logs; wrap in parchment paper. Refrigerate overnight. Heat oven to 350°F. Line several baking sheets with parchment paper. Cut logs into ¼-inch slices. Arrange about 2 inches apart on baking sheets.

4 Bake 10 minutes or until light brown. Cool on baking sheet 1 minute. Place cookies on wire rack; cool completely.

5 dozen

LITTLE FILLED HUNGARIAN COOKIES

BETTE BANJACK
NORRISTOWN, PENNSYLVANIA

1 lb. ground walnuts

½ lb. powdered sugar

2 large egg whites

1 teaspoon milk

1 cup butter

1 (8-oz.) pkg. cream cheese, softened

1 tablespoon sugar

2 cups all-purpose flour

1 In large bowl, combine walnuts, powdered sugar, egg whites and milk; mix until well blended. Set aside.

2 In another large bowl, beat butter and cream cheese at medium speed until well blended. Add sugar; slowly beat in flour. Cover and refrigerate 30 minutes.

3 Heat oven to 350°F. Spray several baking sheets with nonstick cooking spray.

4 Divide dough into 3 balls. Roll out each ball of dough to ¼-inch thickness on powdered-sugar covered work surface. Cut into 3-inch squares.

5 Place 1 teaspoon filling at one side of each square. Roll up dough from filling side. Roll cookies in powdered sugar. Arrange about 2 inches apart on baking sheets. Bake 35 minutes or until golden brown. Cool on wire rack.

6 dozen

TOFFEE CHOCOLATE CHIP COOKIES

NANCY WILKE
HUDSONVILLE, MICHIGAN

3 cups old-fashioned or quick-cooking oats

4 cups all-purpose flour

2 tablespoons baking powder

2 teaspoons baking soda

1 teaspoon salt

3/4 cup butter, softened

2 cups sugar

2 cups packed brown sugar

4 eggs

2 teaspoons vanilla

2 cups semisweet chocolate chips (12 oz.)

1 cup toffee chips

1 cup chopped pecans, toasted

1 Heat oven to 350°F. Line several baking sheets with parchment paper.

2 Place oats in food processor; pulse until finely ground. Set aside.

3 In large bowl, combine flour, baking powder, baking soda and salt; set aside.

4 In another large bowl, beat butter, sugar, brown sugar, eggs and vanilla at medium speed 2 minutes. Add flour mixture; mix until blended. Stir in pulverized oats, chocolate chips, toffee chips and pecans.

5 Drop by rounded teaspoonfuls about 2 inches apart on baking sheets. Bake 6 to 8 minutes or until brown. Cool on wire rack.

4 dozen

CHEESE-FILLED COOKIES

VIVIAN NIKANOW
CHICAGO, ILLINOIS

COOKIES

1 cup butter

4 oz. cream cheese, softened

1 cup sugar

1 egg

1 teaspoon grated lemon peel

1 tablespoon lemon juice

1 teaspoon vanilla

2 1/4 cups all-purpose flour

1 teaspoon baking powder

1/4 cup finely crushed graham-cracker crumbs

CHEESE FILLING

4 oz. cream cheese

2 tablespoons sugar

1/2 teaspoon grated lemon peel

1/2 teaspoon vanilla

1 egg yolk

1 tablespoon half-and-half

1 In large bowl, beat butter, 4 oz. cream cheese and 1 cup sugar at medium speed until well blended. Add egg, 1 teaspoon lemon peel, lemon juice and 1 teaspoon vanilla; mix well. In separate bowl, combine flour and baking powder. Add to cream cheese mixture; blend well. Cover; refrigerate at least 1 hour or until cold and firm.

2 Heat oven to 350°F. Line several baking sheets with parchment paper.

3 To prepare filling, beat 4 oz. cream cheese, 2 tablespoons sugar, 1/2 teaspoon lemon peel, 1/2 teaspoon vanilla, egg yolk and half-and-half at medium speed until smooth. Set aside.

4 Shape dough into 1-inch balls. Roll in graham cracker crumbs. Arrange about 2 inches apart on baking sheets. With finger, make indentation in center of each cookie. Fill with 1/2 teaspoon filling. Bake 20 minutes or until lightly browned. Cool on wire rack. Store in airtight container.

About 4 dozen

ISABELLAS

JANE MORITA
SAN GABRIEL, CALIFORNIA

1 cup butter

$\frac{1}{2}$ cup sugar

1 teaspoon vanilla

1 $\frac{1}{4}$ cups all-purpose flour

1 $\frac{1}{2}$ cups old-fashioned or quick-cooking oats

$\frac{1}{8}$ teaspoon salt

1 $\frac{1}{2}$ cups powdered sugar

1 In large bowl, beat butter and sugar at medium speed until light. Beat in vanilla, flour, oats and salt. Refrigerate 30 minutes or until cold and firm.

2 Heat oven to 350°F. Line several baking sheets with parchment paper.

3 Shape dough into 1-inch balls; place about 2 inches apart on baking sheets. Flatten using crisscross indentations with fork. Bake 12 to 15 minutes or until lightly browned. Sprinkle with powdered sugar, if desired.

2 $\frac{1}{2}$ dozen

MRS. WAGENTI'S FILLED KIFLI COOKIES

PEGGY WINKWORTH
DURANGO, COLORADO

1 cup butter

$\frac{1}{2}$ cup sour cream

2 cups all-purpose flour

1 (4-oz.) jar apricot or raspberry jam

1 egg white, beaten

$\frac{1}{2}$ cup finely chopped nuts

1 In large bowl, beat butter, sour cream and flour at medium speed until blended. Refrigerate dough 1 hour or until cold and firm. Roll dough to $\frac{1}{8}$ inch thickness on floured surface; cut with 3$\frac{1}{2}$-inch round cutter. Place scant teaspoon jam on each round. Fold two sides to middle; squeeze edges together. Beat egg whites until stiff peaks form. Brush cookies with egg whites and sprinkle with nuts.

2 Heat oven to 350°F. Line several baking sheets with parchment paper. Arrange about 2 inches apart on baking sheet. Bake 15 minutes or until lightly browned. Cool on wire rack.

3 to 4 dozen

CORNUCOPIA COOKIES

MARYANN MINICHIELLO
JOHNSTON, RHODE ISLAND

COOKIES

$\frac{1}{4}$ cup melted butter

$\frac{1}{4}$ cup sugar

1 egg

1 teaspoon vanilla

$\frac{1}{2}$ teaspoon almond extract

1 $\frac{1}{3}$ cups all-purpose flour

1 $\frac{1}{2}$ teaspoons baking powder

$\frac{1}{8}$ teaspoon salt

NUT FILLING

$\frac{3}{4}$ cup chopped walnuts

1 tablespoon melted butter

$\frac{1}{2}$ cup chopped pecans

2 tablespoons water

$\frac{1}{3}$ cup sugar

$\frac{1}{4}$ teaspoon maple extract

$\frac{1}{4}$ teaspoon salt

1 Heat oven to 375°F. Line several baking sheets with parchment paper.

2 For cookies, in large bowl, beat $\frac{1}{4}$ cup butter and $\frac{1}{4}$ cup sugar at medium speed until well blended. Add egg, vanilla and almond extract. Combine flour, baking powder and $\frac{1}{8}$ teaspoon salt. Gradually add flour mixture to butter mixture; blend thoroughly.

3 To prepare filling, combine walnuts, melted butter, pecans, water, $\frac{1}{3}$ cup sugar, maple extract and $\frac{1}{16}$ teaspoon salt in large bowl; mix until well combined.

4 Roll out dough on lightly floured surface to $\frac{1}{8}$-inch thickness. Cut with 3-inch round cookie cutter. Place 1 teaspoon nut filling in center of each cookie; shape into cone. Arrange about 2 inches apart on baking sheets. Bake 7 to 10 minutes or until lightly browned. Cool on wire rack.

2 to 3 dozen

LACE COOKIES

LACE COOKIES

CHRIS McBEE
XENIA, OHIO

1 cup all-purpose flour

3/4 cup pecans, chopped

1 cup flaked coconut

1/2 cup light corn syrup

1/2 cup packed brown sugar

1/2 cup butter

1 teaspoon vanilla

1 Heat oven to 350°F. Line several baking sheets with aluminum foil.

2 In large bowl, stir together flour, nuts and coconut; set aside.

3 In medium saucepan, combine corn syrup, brown sugar and butter. Bring mixture to a boil, stirring constantly. Remove from heat; blend in flour mixture and vanilla.

4 Drop by teaspoonfuls about 2 inches apart on baking sheets. Bake 8 to 10 minutes or until set. Cool 3 to 4 minutes on wire rack.

About 4 dozen

TOASTY COCONUT MELTS

VIVIAN NIKANOW
CHICAGO, ILLINOIS

1 cup all-purpose flour

1/2 cup cornstarch

1/2 cup powdered sugar

1 cup butter, softened

1 1/3 cups coconut

1 In large bowl, mix flour, cornstarch and powdered sugar. Blend in butter until smooth. Refrigerate dough until cold and firm.

2 Heat oven to 300°F. Line several baking sheets with parchment paper.

3 Shape dough into 1-inch balls; roll in coconut. Arrange about 2 inches apart on baking sheets. Bake 20 to 25 minutes or until lightly toasted. Cool on wire rack.

3 dozen

FROSTED CASHEW COOKIES

CHERYL PETERSON

COOKIES

2 cups buttermilk baking mix

1 cup packed brown sugar

1/3 cup sour cream

1/4 cup butter, softened

1 egg

1/2 teaspoon vanilla

1 1/2 cups salted cashews, halved

FROSTING

1/3 cup butter

2 cups powdered sugar

1 1/2 teaspoons vanilla

2 tablespoons milk

1 Heat oven to 350°F. Line several baking sheets with parchment paper.

2 In large bowl, beat baking mix, brown sugar, sour cream, 1/4 cup butter, egg and 1/2 teaspoon vanilla at medium speed until blended. Stir in cashews. Drop by rounded teaspoonfuls about 2 inches apart onto baking sheets.

3 Bake 12 to 15 minutes or until no indentation remains when touched. Cool 1 minute; remove from baking sheet. Cool completely on wire rack. Top with frosting.

4 To prepare frosting, melt 1/3 cup butter in saucepan over medium heat until brown; cool. Stir in powdered sugar, 1 1/2 teaspoons vanilla and milk. Beat at medium speed until frosting is smooth. Spread frosting over cooled cookies.

3 1/2 dozen

DAD'S FAVORITE MOLASSES COOKIES

JAYNE HORNSHER
CINCINATTI, OHIO

$^1/_2$ cup butter, softened

1$^1/_2$ cups sugar

$^2/_3$ cup molasses

3 tablespoons grated lemon peel

2 eggs

4 cups all-purpose flour

3 teaspoons baking soda

2 teaspoons ground ginger

1 teaspoon cinnamon

$^1/_2$ teaspoon salt

1 In large bowl, beat butter at medium speed until creamy; gradually add sugar, beating well. Add molasses, lemon peel and eggs; beat well. In medium bowl, combine flour, baking soda, ginger, cinnamon and salt. Gradually add flour mixture to butter mixture; stir well. Cover dough; refrigerate 1 hour.

2 Heat oven to 350°F. Line several baking sheets with parchment paper.

3 Shape dough into 1-inch balls; arrange about 2 inches apart on baking sheets. Bake 12 minutes or until golden. Cool on wire rack.

About 8 dozen

FESTIVE HOLIDAY BISCOTTI

VIVIAN NIKANOW
CHICAGO, ILLINOIS

$^1/_2$ cup butter

1 cup sugar

1 teaspoon baking powder

$^1/_2$ teaspoon baking soda

$^1/_4$ teaspoon salt

4 eggs

1 teaspoon vanilla

$^1/_4$ teaspoon almond extract

2$^1/_4$ cups all-purpose flour

1$^1/_2$ teaspoons anise seeds

$^1/_2$ teaspoon whole fennel seeds

1 cup dried cranberries

$^3/_4$ cup chopped, shelled, whole pistachios

$^1/_2$ cup snipped dried apricots or peaches

1 tablespoon water

1 In large bowl, beat butter, sugar, baking powder, baking soda and salt at medium speed until well blended. Beat in 3 of the eggs, vanilla and almond extract. Add flour, anise seeds, fennel seeds, cranberries, pistachios and apricots; mix well. Cover and refrigerate several hours or overnight.

2 Heat oven to 350°F. Line several baking sheets with parchment paper.

3 Divide dough into thirds. Shape into 3 (12x1$^1/_2$-inch) logs. Place logs onto baking sheets. In small bowl, whisk remaining egg with water. Brush logs with egg mixture. Bake 25 to 30 minutes or until light golden brown. Remove from oven; cool 1 hour.

4 Reduce oven temperature to 325°F. Cut logs into $^1/_2$-inch slices. Place slices cut-side down on baking sheets. Bake 10 minutes. Turn slices over; bake an additional 10 minutes. Cool on wire rack.

4 dozen

BUTTER COOKIES

KIM HILL
HARVEY, ILLINOIS

1/4 cup butter

1/2 cup powdered
sugar

1/2 cup sugar

1/2 cup vegetable oil

1 teaspoon vanilla

1 egg

2 cups all-purpose flour

1 teaspoon baking
soda

1 teaspoon cream
of tartar

1 Heat oven to 375°F. Line several baking sheets
with parchment paper.

2 In large bowl, beat butter, powdered sugar, sugar
and oil at medium speed until well blended. Add
vanilla and egg. In another bowl, mix together flour,
baking soda and cream of tartar; add to butter mixture.

3 Shape dough into 1-inch balls; arrange on baking
sheets about 2 inches apart. Press down with cup.
Bake 10 to 12 minutes or until lightly brown on
edges. Cool on wire rack.

About 6 dozen

SUGAR CUT-OUTS

PEGGY M. YAMAGUCHI-LAZAR
EUGENE, OREGON

1 cup butter, softened

2/3 cup packed brown sugar

1 egg

1 teaspoon vanilla

2 1/2 cups all-purpose flour

1 cup old-fashioned or quick-cooking oats

1 In large bowl, beat butter, brown sugar, egg and
vanilla at medium speed until well blended. Add
flour. Stir in oats. Refrigerate until cold and firm.

2 Heat oven to 350°F. Line several baking sheets
with parchment paper.

3 Roll out dough on floured surface to 1/8-inch
thickness. With 2- to 3-inch cutters, cut out cookies.
With spatula, transfer to baking sheets, arranging
about 2 inches apart.

4 Bake 8 to 10 minutes or until edges are light
brown. Cool on baking sheet 1 minute. Place cookies on wire rack; cool completely.

2 1/2 dozen

PEANUT BUTTER COOKIES

JOYCE QUICK
CANDOR, NEW YORK

1/2 cup sugar

1/2 cup packed brown sugar

1/2 cup peanut butter

1/4 cup shortening

1/4 cup butter

1 egg

1 1/4 cup all-purpose flour

3/4 teaspoon baking soda

1/2 teaspoon baking powder

1/4 teaspoon salt

1 Heat oven to 375°F. Line several baking sheets
with parchment paper.

2 In large bowl, beat sugar, brown sugar, peanut
butter, shortening and butter at medium speed until
blended. Beat in egg, flour, baking soda, baking
powder and salt; mix well.

3 Shape dough into 1-inch balls; arrange about 2
inches apart on baking sheets. Press with tines of
fork in crisscross pattern. Bake 9 to 10 minutes or
until lightly browned at edges. Cool 1 minute on
baking sheet; cool completely on wire rack.

About 3 dozen

BANANA OATMEAL ROCKS

LINDA ZIERDEN
ST. CLOUD, MINNESOTA

1$\frac{1}{2}$ cups all-purpose flour

$\frac{1}{2}$ teaspoon baking soda

1 teaspoon salt

$\frac{1}{4}$ teaspoon nutmeg

$\frac{3}{4}$ teaspoon cinnamon

$\frac{3}{4}$ cup shortening

1 cup sugar

1 egg

1 cup mashed bananas

1$\frac{3}{4}$ cup old-fashioned or quick-cooking oats

$\frac{1}{2}$ cup walnuts

1 Heat oven to 325°F. Line several baking sheets with parchment paper.

2 In large bowl, mix together flour, baking soda, salt, nutmeg and cinnamon.

3 In another large bowl, beat shortening at medium speed until fluffy. Add sugar, egg, bananas, oats and walnuts; beat until blended. Add flour mixture; mix until blended. Drop by teaspoonfuls about 2 inches apart on baking sheets. Bake about 20 minutes or until brown. Cool on wire rack.

About 4 dozen

INSIDE-OUT CHOCOLATE CHIP COOKIES

CHRISTINA POOL
SALEM, OREGON

1 cup sugar

$\frac{3}{4}$ cup packed brown sugar

$\frac{3}{4}$ cup butter, softened

$\frac{1}{2}$ cup shortening

2 eggs

1 teaspoon vanilla

2$\frac{1}{2}$ cups all-purpose flour

$\frac{1}{2}$ cup unsweetened cocoa

1 teaspoon baking soda

$\frac{1}{4}$ teaspoon salt

1$\frac{1}{2}$ cups white chocolate chips (9 oz.)

1 cup chopped nuts, if desired

1 Heat oven to 350°F. Line several baking sheets with parchment paper.

2 In large bowl, beat sugar, brown sugar, butter, shortening, eggs and vanilla at medium speed until well blended. Add flour, cocoa, baking soda, salt, chips and nuts; beat until well blended.

3 Drop dough by rounded teaspoonfuls about 2 inches apart onto baking sheets. Bake 10 to 12 minutes or until set. Cool 2 minutes on baking sheets; cool completely on wire racks.

4 dozen

INSIDE-OUT CHOCOLATE CHIP COOKIES

WALNUT BUTTER COOKIES (SANDWICHED WITH JELLY)

WALNUT BUTTER COOKIES (SANDWICHED WITH JELLY)

JEFFREY A. BUSSE
SHRUB OAK, NEW YORK

1 cup butter, softened

1 cup sugar

3 eggs, separated

1 teaspoon vanilla

$1/8$ teaspoon salt

3 cups all-purpose flour

$1/2$ teaspoon baking powder

$1/2$ lb. walnuts, finely chopped

$1/4$ cup decorative sugar (red or green)

Assorted fruit jellies

1 In large bowl, beat butter at medium speed until fluffy. Beat in sugar, egg yolks, vanilla and salt. Stir in flour and baking powder until well blended. Refrigerate 1 hour.

2 Heat oven to 350°F. Line several baking sheets with parchment paper.

3 Roll out dough to $1/8$=inch thickness; cut out one-half of dough with $2^1/2$-inch round cutters. Cut out remaining dough with a $2^1/2$-inch doughnut cutter. Combine walnuts and decorative sugar. Brush doughnut-shaped cut-outs with egg white; sprinkle with walnut-sugar mixture. Arrange about 2 inches apart on baking sheets. Bake 6 to 7 minutes or until light brown; cool on wire rack.

4 Spread bottom side of round cookies with desired flavor jellies; top with doughnut-shaped cookies, decorated tops up.

About 3 dozen

PEANUTTY FUDGE PUDDLES

TERI HARVEY
CORVALLIS, OREGON

$1^1/4$ cups all-purpose flour

$3/4$ teaspoon baking soda

$1/2$ teaspoon salt

$1/2$ cup sugar

$1/2$ cup packed brown sugar

$1/2$ cup butter, softened

$1/2$ cup peanut butter

1 egg

$1/2$ teaspoon vanilla

FUDGE FILLING

1 cup semisweet chocolate chips (6 oz.)

$2/3$ cup sweetened condensed milk

$1/2$ teaspoon vanilla

$1/4$ cup dry-roasted peanuts

1 Heat oven to 325°F. Spray miniature ($1^3/4$-inch) muffin cups with nonstick cooking spray.

2 In large bowl, combine flour, baking soda and salt; set aside. In another large bowl, beat sugar, brown sugar, butter and peanut butter at medium speed until blended and fluffy. Add egg and $1/2$ teaspoon vanilla. Beat flour mixture into butter mixture. Stir well. Refrigerate 1 hour.

3 Shape dough into 1-inch balls. Place in muffin cups. Bake 14 to 16 minutes or until lightly browned. Remove from oven and immediately press "wells" into center of each cookie with melon baller. Cool in pan 5 minutes. Cool completely on wire rack.

4 In microwave-safe bowl, melt chips in microwave. Stir milk and $1/2$ teaspoon vanilla into melted chips until smooth. Place a few peanuts into each cookie's "well" and fill with fudge filling. Allow to cool on counter until firm. Store in airtight container.

4 dozen

CRISPY CHOCOLATE-BUTTERSCOTCH COOKIES

DAWN HALLOWELL
PORTLAND, MAINE

1 1/2 cups all-purpose flour

1/2 teaspoon baking soda

1/2 teaspoon salt

1/2 cup butter, softened

1/2 cup vegetable oil

1/2 cup sugar

1/2 cup packed brown sugar

1 egg

1 teaspoon vanilla

1 cup butterscotch chips (6 oz.)

1 cup semisweet chocolate chips (6 oz.)

1/2 cup old-fashioned or quick-cooking oats

1/2 cup crushed cereal flakes

1/2 cup flaked coconut

1/2 cup chopped pecans

1 Heat oven to 350°F. Line several baking sheets with parchment paper.

2 In small bowl, combine flour, baking soda and salt; set aside. In large bowl, beat butter, oil, sugar, brown sugar, egg and vanilla at medium speed until well blended and fluffy. Gradually beat in flour mixture. Stir in chips, oats, cereal, coconut and nuts.

3 Drop by rounded tablespoonfuls about 2 inches apart onto baking sheets. Bake 10 to 14 minutes or until edges are crisp but centers are still slightly soft. Let stand 2 minutes on baking sheets; remove to wire racks to cool completely.

3 1/2 dozen

MOCHA NUT BUTTERBALLS

VIVIAN NIKANOW
CHICAGO, ILLINOIS

1 cup butter, softened

1/2 cup sugar

2 teaspoons vanilla

2 teaspoons coffee granules

1/3 cup unsweetened cocoa

1 2/3 cups all-purpose flour

2 cups finely chopped pecans or walnuts

1/2 cup powdered sugar

1 Heat oven to 325°F. Line several baking sheets with parchment paper.

2 In large bowl, beat butter, sugar and vanilla at medium speed until light and fluffy. Add coffee, cocoa and flour; beat until blended. Add nuts and mix well. Shape dough into 1-inch balls. Arrange on baking sheets about 1/2 inch apart.

3 Bake 15 minutes or until cookies crack slightly. Cool cookies on wire rack. Roll cookies in powdered sugar.

4 dozen

CHEWY OATMEAL COOKIES

GINGER HEITMAN
CAMP POINT, ILLINOIS

3/4 cup butter-flavored shortening	1 cup all-purpose flour
1 1/4 cups packed brown sugar	1/2 teaspoon baking soda
1 egg	1/2 teaspoon salt
1/3 cup milk	1/4 teaspoon cinnamon
1 1/2 teaspoons vanilla	1 cup raisins
3 cups old-fashioned or quick-cooking oats	1 cup chopped nuts

1 Heat oven to 375°F. Line several baking sheets with parchment paper.

2 In large bowl, beat shortening, brown sugar, egg, milk and vanilla at medium speed until blended and fluffy. Add oats, flour, baking soda, salt, cinnamon, raisins and nuts; stir well.

3 Roll into 1-inch balls. Arrange about 2 inches apart on baking sheets. Bake 10 to 12 minutes or until edges are light brown. Cool on wire rack.

3 1/2 dozen

CHOCOLATE CHIP CRISPY RICE COOKIES

LORRIE GIBSON
PORTSMOUTH, NEW HAMPSHIRE

2 cups all-purpose flour

¼ teaspoon salt

½ teaspoon baking soda

½ cup packed brown sugar

¾ cup butter, softened

1 egg

2 teaspoons vanilla

1 cup crispy rice cereal

1½ cups semisweet chocolate chips (9 oz.)

1 Heat oven to 300°F. Line several baking sheets with parchment paper.

2 In medium bowl, combine flour, salt and baking soda; set aside. In large bowl, beat brown sugar and butter at medium speed until well blended. Add egg and vanilla; beat at medium speed until light and fluffy. Add flour mixture, cereal and chips. Beat at low speed just until combined.

3 Drop by rounded tablespoonfuls about 2 inches apart onto baking sheets. Bake 20 minutes. Immediately transfer cookies with spatula to wire rack. Store in airtight container.

3 dozen

ROYAL COCONUT COOKIES

RAMONA N. KLOPPING
OMAHA, NEBRASKA

1¼ cups all-purpose flour

1 teaspoon baking powder

1 teaspoon baking soda

½ teaspoon salt

½ cup shortening

½ cup sugar

½ cup packed brown sugar

1 egg

1 cup old-fashioned, or quick-cooking oats

1 cup flaked coconut

½ teaspoon vanilla

1 Heat oven to 350°F. Line several baking sheets with parchment paper.

2 In large bowl, mix together flour, baking powder, baking soda and salt; set aside. In another large bowl, combine shortening, sugar and brown sugar; stir until soft. Add egg, oats, coconut and vanilla; beat at medium speed until well blended. Beat in flour mixture.

3 Shape dough into 1-inch balls; arrange about 2 inches apart on baking sheets. Bake 12 minutes or until brown. Cool on wire rack.

3 dozen

TURN-OF-THE-CENTURY OATMEAL COOKIES

PEGGY M. YAMAGUCHI-LAZAR
EUGENE, OREGON

½ cup butter, softened

2 eggs

1 cup sugar

1 cup packed brown sugar

2½ cups all-purpose flour

1 cup old-fashioned or quick-cooking oats

¼ cup toasted wheat germ

¼ teaspoon baking soda

½ teaspoon cream of tartar

1 teaspoon vanilla

1 Heat oven to 375°F. Line several baking sheets with parchment paper.

2 In large bowl, beat butter, eggs, sugar and brown sugar at medium speed until well blended. In another large bowl, mix flour, oats, wheat germ, baking soda and cream of tartar. Combine butter mixture and flour mixture; stir in vanilla until well blended. Add nuts or raisins, if desired.

3 Roll into 1-inch balls; arrange about 2 inches apart on baking sheets. Bake 10 minutes or until edges are light brown. Cool on wire rack.

5 dozen

SOUR CREAM CUT-OUT COOKIES

SOUR CREAM CUT-OUT COOKIES

CHRIS MCBEE
XENIA, OHIO

6 cups all-purpose flour

1 teaspoon baking soda

$\frac{1}{2}$ teaspoon nutmeg

$\frac{1}{2}$ cup butter

$\frac{1}{2}$ cup shortening

2 cups sugar

3 eggs

1 cup sour cream

1 In large bowl, combine flour, baking soda and nutmeg; set aside. In another large bowl, beat butter, shortening, sugar and eggs at medium speed until well blended and fluffy. Add sour cream and flour mixture; beat until well blended. Refrigerate 1 to 2 hours.

2 Heat oven to 375°F. Line several baking sheets with parchment paper.

3 Roll out dough to $\frac{1}{4}$ inch thickness on lightly floured surface. With 2- to 3-inch assorted cutters, cut out cookies. With spatula, transfer cookies to baking sheets, arranging about 2 inches apart.

4 Bake 8 to 10 minutes or until edges are light brown. Cool on baking sheet 1 minute. Place cookies on wire rack; cool completely.

About 4 dozen

MOM MANGES' RAISIN COOKIES

JUDY MANGES
HORNELL, NEW YORK

2 cups raisins

1 cup water

1 cup shortening

1$\frac{3}{4}$ cups sugar

2 eggs, lightly beaten

1 teaspoon vanilla

3$\frac{1}{2}$ cups all-purpose flour

1 teaspoon baking powder

1 teaspoon baking soda

1 teaspoon salt

$\frac{1}{2}$ teaspoon cinnamon

$\frac{1}{2}$ teaspoon nutmeg

$\frac{1}{2}$ cup chopped walnuts

1 cup semisweet chocolate chips (6 oz.)

1 Heat oven to 350°F. Line several baking sheets with parchment paper.

2 In small saucepan, combine raisins and water; bring to a boil. Cook 3 minutes. Cool; do not drain.

3 In large bowl, beat shortening at medium speed until fluffy; gradually beat in sugar, eggs and vanilla. In another large bowl, combine flour, baking powder, baking soda, salt, cinnamon and nutmeg; gradually add to shortening mixture and blend thoroughly. Stir in walnuts and chips.

4 Drop by teaspoonfuls about 2 inches apart on baking sheets. Bake 12 to 14 minutes or until edges are light brown. Cool on wire rack.

About 6 dozen

WHITE CLOUD COOKIES

CYNTHIA POLVADO
AUSTIN, TEXAS

1³/4 cups all-purpose flour

³/4 teaspoon baking soda

¹/4 teaspoon salt

²/3 cup butter, softened

1 cup packed brown sugar

1 teaspoon vanilla

1 egg

¹/2 cup sour cream

2 cups white chocolate chips (12 oz.)

1 cup chopped pecans

1 Heat oven to 375°F. Line several baking sheets with parchment paper.

2 In large bowl, mix flour, baking soda and salt; set aside. In another large bowl, beat butter, brown sugar and vanilla at medium speed until well blended and fluffy. Add egg, sour cream and flour mixture; blend thoroughly. Stir in chips and pecans.

3 Drop by teaspoonfuls about 2 inches apart onto baking sheets. Bake 10 to 13 minutes or until edges are light brown. Cool on baking sheets 2 minutes; place on wire racks. Cool completely.

About 4 dozen

CHEWY BROWNIE COOKIES

JENNIFER GULLO
RENO, NEVADA

²/3 cup shortening

1¹/2 cups packed brown sugar

1 tablespoon water

1 teaspoon vanilla

2 eggs

1¹/2 cups all-purpose flour

¹/3 cup unsweetened cocoa

¹/2 teaspoon salt

¹/4 teaspoon baking soda

2 cups semisweet chocolate chips (12 oz.)

1 Heat oven to 375°F. Line several baking sheets with parchment paper.

2 In large bowl, beat shortening, brown sugar, water and vanilla at medium speed until well blended. Add eggs; beat well. In small bowl, combine flour, cocoa, salt and baking soda; gradually add to shortening mixture, beating on low speed just until blended. Stir in chocolate chips.

3 Drop by rounded tablespoonfuls about 2 inches apart onto baking sheets. Bake 7 to 9 minutes or until cookies are set. Cool 2 minutes; remove to wire racks.

3 dozen

BEST EVER CHOCOLATE CHIP COOKIES

LOLA M. CARPENTER
FREDERICKTOWN, MISSOURI

$2\frac{1}{4}$ cups all-purpose flour

1 teaspoon baking soda

$\frac{1}{4}$ teaspoon salt

$\frac{3}{4}$ cup butter, softened

$\frac{1}{4}$ cup shortening

$\frac{3}{4}$ cup sugar

$\frac{3}{4}$ cup packed brown sugar

2 eggs

1 teaspoon vanilla

2 cups semisweet chocolate chips (12 oz.)

1 Heat oven to 375°F. Line several baking sheets with parchment paper.

2 In large bowl, combine flour, baking soda and salt; set aside. In another large bowl, beat butter and shortening at medium speed until well blended and fluffy. Gradually add sugar, brown sugar, eggs and vanilla; beat until well blended. Add flour mixture to butter mixture; mix well. Stir in chocolate chips.

3 Drop dough by heaping teaspoonfuls about 2 inches apart onto baking sheets. Bake 9 to 11 minutes. Cool slightly on cookie sheets; cool completely on wire rack.

About $6\frac{1}{2}$ dozen

MALTED CHOCOLATE CHIP COOKIES

BRENDA VAN TINE
CANTON, ILLINOIS

$\frac{1}{2}$ cup butter

$\frac{1}{2}$ cup shortening

1 cup packed brown sugar

$\frac{1}{2}$ cup sugar

2 eggs

1 teaspoon almond extract

2 teaspoons vanilla

$\frac{1}{2}$ teaspoon salt

2 teaspoons baking soda

$\frac{1}{2}$ cup chocolate syrup

$\frac{1}{2}$ cup malted milk powder

$\frac{1}{2}$ cup old-fashioned or quick-cooking oats

$3\frac{1}{2}$ cups all-purpose flour

2 cups semisweet chocolate chips (12 oz.)

1 Heat oven to 325°F. Line several baking sheets with parchment paper.

2 In large bowl, beat butter, shortening, brown sugar and sugar at medium speed until well blended and fluffy. Add eggs, almond extract, vanilla, salt, baking soda, chocolate syrup and malted milk powder; beat until well blended. Add oats and flour; beat until well blended. Stir in chocolate chips.

3 Drop dough by rounded teaspoonfuls about 2 inches apart onto baking sheets. Bake 7 to 10 minutes or until light brown and set. Cool on wire racks.

About 4 dozen

INDULGENT BARS

& BROWNIES

KEY LIME BARS (page 80)

LEMON BARS

MARIJO WHITE
MINNETONKA, MINNESOTA

2$\frac{1}{4}$ cups all-purpose flour

1 cup butter

1$\frac{1}{2}$ cups powdered sugar

4 eggs, beaten

2 cups sugar

1 teaspoon baking powder

6 tablespoons fresh lemon juice

Powdered sugar

1 Heat oven to 350°F.

2 In medium bowl, mix 2 cups of the flour, butter and powdered sugar until crumbly. Press mixture into 13x9-inch pan; bake 20 minutes.

3 In another medium bowl, combine eggs, sugar, remaining ¼ cup flour, baking powder and lemon juice; mix until well blended. Pour mixture over baked crust. Bake an additional 30 minutes or until edges are light golden brown and filling is set. Cool completely. Sprinkle with powdered sugar. Cut into bars. Store in refrigerator.

2 dozen bars

FUDGY BROWNIES

KATHY KIRKLAND
DENHAM SPRINGS, LOUISIANA

BROWNIES

1$\frac{1}{3}$ cups all-purpose flour

1 teaspoon baking powder

$\frac{1}{2}$ teaspoon salt

1 cup butter, melted

1 cup unsweetened cocoa

2 cups sugar

4 eggs

1$\frac{1}{2}$ teaspoons vanilla

1 cup chopped nuts

FROSTING

3 tablespoons melted butter

$\frac{1}{2}$ cup unsweetened cocoa

$\frac{1}{2}$ cup unsweetened cocoa

$\frac{1}{4}$ cup milk

$\frac{1}{2}$ teaspoon vanilla

2 cups powdered sugar

1 Heat oven to 350°F. Spray 13x9-inch pan with nonstick cooking spray.

2 In large bowl, combine flour, baking powder, salt and butter. Stir in 1 cup cocoa, sugar, eggs and 1$\frac{1}{2}$ teaspoons vanilla; mix together well. Add nuts. Pour mixture into pan.

3 Bake 30 to 35 minutes or until set. Cool completely.

4 In medium bowl, combine 3 tablespoons melted butter with $\frac{1}{2}$ cup cocoa; blend in milk, $\frac{1}{2}$ teaspoon vanilla and 2 cups powdered sugar. Spread frosting over cooled brownies.

2 dozen brownies

BUTTERSCOTCH SUNDAE BARS

DIANA HARRIS
HENDERSON, MICHIGAN

CRUST

1/3 cup butter

1 teaspoon vanilla

1/2 teaspoon salt

1 cup all-purpose flour

2 tablespoons milk

1/2 cup powdered sugar

FILLING

1 cup butterscotch chips (6 oz.)

2 tablespoons milk

2 tablespoons butter

1/2 cup powdered sugar

1/2 cup chopped nuts

TOPPING

1/2 cup semisweet chocolate chips (3 oz.)

3 tablespoons milk

1/2 cup powdered sugar

2 tablespoons butter

1 Heat oven to 350°F.

2 In medium bowl, combine 1/3 cup butter, vanilla, salt, flour, 2 tablespoons milk and 1/2 cup powdered sugar; mix until well blended. Pour mixture into 8-inch square pan. Bake 20 minutes.

3 To prepare filling, melt butterscotch chips with 2 tablespoons milk in medium saucepan. Stir in 2 tablespoons butter, 1/2 cup powdered sugar and nuts; pour mixture over crust.

4 In another medium saucepan, melt chocolate chips with 3 tablespoons milk; add 1/2 cup powdered sugar and 2 tablespoons butter. Pour mixture over butterscotch layer. Refrigerate until set.

1 dozen bars

RASPBERRY FUDGE BROWNIES

VIVIAN NIKANOW
CHICAGO, ILLINOIS

1/3 cup butter

3 (1-oz.) squares semisweet chocolate

2 eggs

1 cup sugar

1 teaspoon vanilla

3/4 cup all-purpose flour

1/4 teaspoon baking powder

1/8 teaspoon salt

1/2 cup sliced or slivered almonds

1/2 cup seedless raspberry preserves

1 cup semisweet chocolate chips (6 oz.)

1 Heat oven to 350°F. Spray 8-inch square pan with nonstick cooking spray.

2 In small saucepan, melt butter and chocolate over low heat; set aside. In large bowl, combine eggs, sugar and vanilla; beat at medium speed until light and fluffy. Beat in chocolate mixture. Stir in flour, baking powder and salt just until blended.

3 Spread three-fourths of mixture in pan; sprinkle with almonds. Bake 10 minutes. Remove from oven; spread preserves over almonds. Carefully spoon remaining batter evenly over preserves.

4 Bake an additional 25 to 30 minutes or until top feels firm to the touch. Remove from oven; sprinkle with chocolate chips. Let stand a few minutes until chips melt. Cool in pan on wire rack. When chocolate is set, cut into 2-inch squares.

16 brownies

MOM'S ANGEL DREAM DESSERT

PEGGY WINKWORTH
DURANGO, COLORADO

1 cup plus 2 tablespoons all-purpose flour

1/2 cup butter

1 1/4 cups plus 2 tablespoons packed brown sugar

2 eggs, beaten

1 teaspoon baking powder

1 cup chopped nuts

1 cup coconut or raisins

1 teaspoon vanilla

1 Heat oven to 350°F.

2 In medium bowl, combine 1 cup of the flour, butter and 2 tablespoons of the brown sugar; mix until well blended. Press mixture into 8-inch square pan; bake 10 minutes.

3 In another medium bowl, combine remaining 1 1/4 cups brown sugar, eggs, remaining 2 tablespoons flour, baking powder, nuts, coconut and vanilla; mix until well blended. Spread mixture over baked crust. Bake an additional 20 to 25 minutes or until edges are light golden brown and filling is set. Cool in pan. Cut into bars. Store in refrigerator.

16 bars

QUICK APRICOT BARS

RUBY MONTGOMERY
HAVELOCK, NORTH CAROLINA

3/4 cup butter

1 cup packed brown sugar

1 3/4 cups all-purpose flour

1/2 teaspoon salt

1/2 teaspoon baking soda

1 1/2 cups old-fashioned or quick-cooking oats

1 (8-oz.) jar apricot jam

1 cup chopped walnuts

1 Heat oven to 400°F. Spray 13x9-inch pan with nonstick cooking spray.

2 In medium bowl, beat butter and brown sugar at medium speed until well blended. Combine flour, salt and baking soda; add to butter mixture. Add oats; blend well. Press one-half of crust mixture into pan. Press down firmly. Stir jam and walnuts together. Spread jam mixture evenly over crust. Press remaining one-half crust mixture evenly over filling.

3 Bake 20 to 25 minutes or until golden brown. Cool in pan on wire rack. Cut into 2x1-inch bars. Store in airtight container.

4 dozen bars

O'HARRA BARS

SUSIE HARTSELL
COLUMBIA, SOUTH CAROLINA

1 cup sugar

1 cup light corn syrup

1 1/2 cups crunchy peanut butter

4 cups toasted rice cereal

1 cup butterscotch chips (6 oz.)

1 cup semisweet chocolate chips (6 oz.)

1 Spray 13x9-inch pan with nonstick cooking spray.

2 In medium saucepan, bring sugar and syrup to a rolling boil. Add peanut butter. Pour mixture over cereal. Press mixture into pan. In medium saucepan, melt butterscotch and chocolate chips over low heat, stirring frequently, until smooth. Spread melted chips over bars. Let stand overnight. Cut into bars.

2 dozen bars

QUICK APRICOT BARS

PUMPKIN TREATS

TAMMY RAYNES
NATCHITOCHES, LOUISIANA

1¾ cups all-purpose flour

⅓ cup packed brown sugar

⅓ cup sugar

1 cup butter

1 cup chopped pecans

1 (27-oz.) jar mincemeat

1 (15-oz.) can pumpkin

1 (14-oz.) can sweetened condensed milk

2 eggs

1 teaspoon cinnamon

½ teaspoon allspice

½ teaspoon salt

1 Heat oven to 425°F.

2 In medium bowl, combine flour, brown sugar and sugar. Cut butter into flour mixture using pastry blender or two knives until mixture crumbles. Stir in pecans. Reserve 1½ cups crumb mixture; press remaining crumb mixture in bottom and halfway up sides of 15½x10½x1-inch baking pan. Spoon mincemeat over crust.

3 In another bowl, combine pumpkin, milk, eggs, cinnamon, allspice and salt; mix until well blended. Pour mixture over mincemeat. Top with reserved crumb mixture.

4 Bake 15 minutes. Reduce oven temperature to 350°F; bake an additional 40 minutes or until golden brown around edges. Cool in pan. Cut into bars and serve warm or at room temperature. Store in refrigerator.

10 to 12 bars

CRUNCHY FUDGE SANDWICHES

KATHIE WELLER
BARNUM, MINNESOTA

1 cup butterscotch chips (6 oz.)

½ cup peanut butter

4 cups crispy rice cereal

1 cup semisweet chocolate chips (6 oz.)

½ cup powdered sugar

2 tablespoons butter

1 tablespoon water

1 Spray 8-inch square pan with nonstick cooking spray.

2 In medium saucepan, melt butterscotch chips and peanut butter over very low heat, stirring constantly until smooth. Stir in cereal. Press one-half of mixture in pan; refrigerate 30 minutes or until set. Set remaining mixture aside.

3 In medium saucepan, melt chocolate chips over very low heat. Stir in powdered sugar, butter and water, stirring constantly until smooth. Spread over cereal mixture. Spread remaining cereal mixture evenly over chocolate layer; press in gently. Refrigerate 1 hour or until firm.

15 squares

PEANUT BUTTER CHOCOLATE GRANOLA BARS

MELISSA JOLLANDS
BELMONT, MICHIGAN

1 (16-oz.) box granola cereal

1 cup corn syrup

1 cup sugar

1 cup peanut butter

1 teaspoon vanilla

1 cup semisweet chocolate chips (6 oz.)

1 Line 13x9-inch pan with parchment paper.

2 Spread cereal evenly in pan. In medium saucepan, bring corn syrup and sugar to a boil. When sugar is dissolved, remove from heat; add peanut butter and vanilla. Mix and pour over cereal; mix thoroughly in pan. Sprinkle with chocolate chips. Refrigerate until set.

2 dozen bars

BEST ZUCCHINI BARS

FANNIE KLINE
MILLERSBURG, OHIO

BARS

2 cups sugar

1 cup vegetable oil

3 eggs

2 cups all-purpose flour

1 teaspoon cinnamon

1 teaspoon salt

2 teaspoons baking soda

$\frac{1}{4}$ teaspoon baking powder

1 teaspoon vanilla

2 cups shredded zucchini

1 small carrot, shredded

$\frac{3}{4}$ cup old-fashioned or quick-cooking oats

1 cup chopped walnuts

ICING

$\frac{1}{2}$ cup butter

1 (3-oz.) pkg. cream cheese

$\frac{1}{2}$ teaspoon almond extract

2 teaspoons vanilla

3 cups powdered sugar

1 Heat oven to 350°F. Spray 15$\frac{1}{2}$x10$\frac{1}{2}$x1-inch baking pan with nonstick cooking spray.

2 In medium bowl, combine 2 cups sugar, oil and eggs; beat well. In another bowl, combine flour, cinnamon, salt, baking soda and baking powder. Add flour mixture to egg mixture; beat 1 minute. Add 1 teaspoon vanilla. Fold in zucchini, carrot, oats and nuts. Pour mixture into pan. Bake 15 to 20 minutes; cool in pan.

3 To prepare icing, beat butter in medium bowl at medium speed until soft. Add cream cheese, almond extract, 2 teaspoons vanilla and powdered sugar; mix until smooth. Spread icing over bars. Store in refrigerator.

2 dozen bars

FUDGY MOCHA BROWNIES WITH A CRUST

VIVIAN NIKANOW
CHICAGO, ILLINOIS

BROWNIES

1$\frac{1}{4}$ cups all-purpose flour

1$\frac{3}{4}$ cups sugar

$\frac{1}{4}$ cup butter

1 (14-oz.) can sweetened condensed milk

$\frac{1}{2}$ cup unsweetened cocoa

1 egg

2 tablespoons coffee-flavored liqueur

1 teaspoon vanilla

$\frac{1}{2}$ teaspoon baking powder

$\frac{3}{4}$ cup chopped nuts

FROSTING

3 tablespoons butter

3 tablespoons unsweetened cocoa

1 tablespoon water

1 tablespoon coffee-flavored liqueur

1$\frac{1}{2}$ cups powdered sugar

1 Heat oven to 350°F.

2 In medium bowl, combine 1 cup of the flour and $\frac{1}{4}$ cup of the sugar; cut in $\frac{1}{4}$ cup butter using pastry blender or two knives until crumbly. Press mixture firmly into bottom of 13x9-inch pan. Bake 15 minutes.

3 Meanwhile, combine milk, ½ cup cocoa, egg, remaining $\frac{1}{4}$ cup flour, 2 tablespoons liqueur, vanilla and baking powder; mix until well blended. Stir in nuts. Spread mixture evenly over crust.

4 Bake 15 minutes or until center is set. Set aside. To prepare frosting, melt 3 tablespoons butter over low heat in small saucepan. Add 3 tablespoons cocoa and water, stirring constantly until mixture thickens (do not boil). Remove from heat; add 1 tablespoon liqueur. Gradually add 1$\frac{1}{2}$ cups powdered sugar, beating until smooth. Add additional water, 1 teaspoon at a time, until desired consistency.

5 Drizzle with frosting; cut into squares. Store tightly covered at room temperature.

3 dozen brownies

GOOEY PEANUT BUTTER BARS

KIMBERLY HAYES
OKLAHOMA CITY, OKLAHOMA

2 cups butter

1 cup sugar

1 cup packed brown sugar

2 eggs

2 cups peanut butter

2 teaspoons vanilla

2 cups all-purpose flour

$1/2$ teaspoon baking powder

$1/2$ cup chopped pecans or walnuts

$1/2$ cup semisweet chocolate chips (3 oz.)

$1/2$ cup white chocolate chips (3 oz.)

$1/2$ cup butterscotch chips (3 oz.)

1 Heat oven to 350°F. Line 13x9-inch pan with aluminum foil.

2 In large bowl, combine butter, sugar and brown sugar until well blended. Add eggs and blend again. Add peanut butter and vanilla, blending well.

3 In another bowl, combine flour and baking powder. Stir into peanut butter mixture. Spread batter evenly into pan. Sprinkle nuts and chips evenly over top. Bake 30 to 35 minutes or until center is firm. Cool completely on wire rack. Cut into 2x1-inch bars.

4 dozen bars

SENSATIONAL MINT BROWNIES

CHERYL PETERSON

$1\frac{1}{2}$ cups melted butter

3 cups sugar

1 tablespoon vanilla

5 eggs

2 cups all-purpose flour

1 cup unsweetened cocoa

1 teaspoon baking powder

1 teaspoon salt

24 ($1\frac{1}{2}$-inch) chocolate-covered peppermint patties

1 Heat oven to 350°F. Spray 13x9-inch pan with nonstick cooking spray.

2 In large bowl, whisk together butter, sugar and vanilla. Add eggs; stir until well blended. Stir in flour, cocoa, baking powder and salt; blend well. Spread remaining batter in pan, reserving 2 cups batter. Arrange peppermint patties in single layer over batter about $1/2$ inch apart. Spread reserved 2 cups batter over patties.

3 Bake 50 to 55 minutes or until brownies begin to pull away from sides of pan. Cool completely in pan. Cut into squares.

3 dozen brownies

CARAMEL CANDY BARS

VIVIAN NIKANOW
CHICAGO, ILLINOIS

1 (14-oz.) pkg. vanilla caramels

1/3 cup milk

2 cups all-purpose flour

2 cups old-fashioned or quick-cooking oats

1 1/2 cups packed brown sugar

1 teaspoon baking soda

1/2 teaspoon salt

1 egg

1 cup butter, softened

1 cup semisweet chocolate chips (6 oz.)

1 cup chopped walnuts or dry roasted peanuts

1 Heat oven to 350°F. Spray 13x9-inch pan with nonstick cooking spray.

2 In medium saucepan, heat caramels and milk over low heat, stirring frequently, until smooth. Remove from heat.

3 In large bowl, combine flour, oats, brown sugar, baking soda, salt, egg and butter; stir until crumbly. Press one-half of mixture in pan. Bake 10 minutes.

4 Sprinkle crust with chocolate chips and walnuts; drizzle with caramel mixture. Sprinkle remaining flour mixture over top.

5 Bake 20 to 25 minutes or until golden brown. Loosen edges from sides of pan with sharp knife. Cut into 2x1-inch bars.

4 1/2 dozen bars

PEANUT BUTTER BROWNIES

KATHY BALL
ARLINGTON HEIGHTS, ILLINOIS

6 tablespoons unsalted butter

1/2 cup chunky peanut butter

1 1/4 cups packed brown sugar

2 large eggs

2 teaspoons vanilla

3/4 cup all-purpose flour

1 teaspoon baking powder

4 (1-oz.) squares semisweet chocolate, coarsely chopped

1 Heat oven to 350°F. Spray 8-inch square pan with nonstick cooking spray.

2 In medium bowl, beat butter and peanut butter at low speed until well blended. Add brown sugar, eggs and vanilla; mix well. Beat in flour and baking powder; stir in chocolate. Spread mixture into pan.

3 Bake 30 to 35 minutes or until golden brown. Cool completely in pan on wire rack before cutting.

24 bars

BABY RUTH BARS

BEATRICE A. MONEYPENNY
SUFFOLK, VIRGINIA

4 cups old-fashioned or quick-cooking oats

1 cup packed brown sugar

1/4 cup light corn syrup

2/3 cup butter, melted

1/4 cup plus 2/3 cup chunky peanut butter

1 teaspoon vanilla

1 cup butterscotch chips (6 oz.)

1 cup semisweet chocolate chips (6 oz.)

1 Heat oven to 400°F. Spray 15 1/2x10 1/2x1-inch baking pan with nonstick cooking spray.

2 In large bowl, combine oats, brown sugar, corn syrup, butter, 1/4 cup of the peanut butter and vanilla; stir together until well blended. Spread mixture into pan. Bake 12 minutes.

3 In small saucepan, melt chips and remaining 2/3 cup peanut butter over low heat. Spread mixture over baked layer. Refrigerate until set. Cut into bars.

2 dozen bars

RHUBARB MERINGUE

TRUDEE BILLO
GALION, OHIO

1 1/2 cups all-purpose flour

1/2 cup butter, softened

5 tablespoons powdered sugar

3 eggs

2 cups sugar

1 teaspoon baking powder

3 cups rhubarb, chopped in 1/2-inch pieces

1 Heat oven to 350°F. Spray 8-inch square pan with nonstick cooking spray.

2 In medium bowl, combine 1 cup of the flour, butter and powdered sugar; mix until well blended. Press mixture into pan; bake 15 minutes.

3 In another medium bowl, beat eggs, sugar, remaining 1/2 cup flour and baking powder; mix until well blended. Stir in rhubarb. Spread mixture on top of baked crust. Bake an additional 45 minutes or until golden brown. Cool in pan. Cut into 2-inch squares.

16 bars

MAPLE BUTTERSCOTCH BROWNIES

TAMMY RAYNES
NATCHITOCHES, LOUISIANA

1/2 cup butter, melted

1 1/2 cups packed brown sugar

1 1/2 teaspoons maple flavoring

2 eggs

1 1/2 cups all-purpose flour

1 teaspoon baking powder

1 cup chopped walnuts

1 Heat oven to 350°F. Spray 8-inch square pan with nonstick cooking spray.

2 In large bowl, beat butter and brown sugar at medium speed until fluffy. Add maple flavoring and eggs, one at a time, beating well after each addition.

3 In small bowl, combine flour and baking powder; add to butter mixture. Stir in walnuts. Pour mixture into pan. Bake 30 minutes or just until brownies begin to pull away from sides of pan. Cool in pan on wire rack. Dust with powdered sugar, if desired. Cut into 2-inch squares.

16 brownies

SNICKERS BARS

PEGGY KIRBY
SANTA CRUZ, CALIFORNIA

2 cups semisweet chocolate chips (12 oz.)

2 cups butterscotch chips (12 oz.)

3/4 cup creamy peanut butter

1/4 cup butter

1 cup sugar

1/4 cup evaporated milk

1 1/2 cups marshmallow crème

1 teaspoon vanilla

1 1/2 cups chopped salted peanuts

1 Line 13x9-inch pan with aluminum foil. Spray with nonstick cooking spray.

2 In small saucepan, combine 1/4 cup of the chocolate chips, 1/4 cup of the butterscotch chips and 1/4 cup of the peanut butter; stir over low heat until melted and smooth. Spread mixture into bottom of pan. Refrigerate until set.

3 In heavy saucepan, heat butter over medium-high heat until melted. Add sugar and milk; bring to a boil. Stir 5 minutes; remove from heat. Stir in marshmallow crème, 1/4 cup of the peanut butter and vanilla. Add peanuts. Spread marshmallow mixture over bottom layer. Refrigerate until set.

4 In another saucepan, combine remaining 1 3/4 cup chocolate chips, remaining 1 3/4 cup butterscotch chips and remaining 1/4 cup peanut butter; stir over low heat until melted and smooth. Pour over marshmallow layer. Refrigerate at least 1 hour. Cut into 1-inch squares. Store in refrigerator.

4 dozen bars

CREAM CHEESE BROWNIES

KAREN COLEMAN
FORT FAIRFIELD, MAINE

1 (8-oz.) pkg. cream cheese

1⅓ cups sugar

3 eggs

¼ teaspoon almond extract

2 (1-oz.) squares semisweet chocolate

½ cup butter

¾ cup all-purpose flour

½ teaspoon salt

½ teaspoon baking powder

½ cup chopped nuts

1 Heat oven to 350°F. Spray 8-inch square pan with nonstick cooking spray.

2 In large bowl, beat cream cheese, ⅓ cup of the sugar, 1 of the eggs and almond extract; set aside. In small saucepan, heat chocolate and butter over medium-high heat until melted; set aside.

3 In another large bowl, beat remaining 2 eggs and remaining 1 cup sugar with chocolate mixture. In small bowl, combine flour, salt and baking powder; stir into chocolate mixture and mix well.

4 Pour one-half of chocolate mixture into pan. Spread cream cheese mixture over top. Pour remaining batter over cream cheese and sprinkle with nuts. Bake 40 minutes or until set. Cool in pan. Cut into bars.

2 dozen brownies

KEY LIME BARS

CHARLOTTE WARD
HILTON HEAD, SOUTH CAROLINA

BARS

2 cups all-purpose flour

1 cup butter, softened

½ cup powdered sugar

FILLING

2 cups sugar

¼ cup all-purpose flour

1 teaspoon baking powder

4 eggs

½ cup fresh or bottled Key lime juice

¼ cup grated Key or regular lime peel

Powdered sugar

1 Heat oven to 350°F.

2 In medium bowl, combine 2 cups flour, butter and ½ cup powdered sugar; mix thoroughly. Press mixture into 13x9-inch pan. Bake 10 minutes. Set aside.

3 In large bowl, combine 2 cups sugar, ¼ cup flour, baking powder and eggs; mix until well blended. Gently stir in lime juice and peel. Carefully pour over hot crust. Bake an additional 25 to 30 minutes or until edges are light brown and filling is set. Cool completely on wire rack; sprinkle with powdered sugar. Cut into 1½-inch squares. Store in refrigerator.

About 4 dozen bars

KEY LIME BARS

ALMOND-FLAVORED LIQUEUR BROWNIES

CHRIS McBEE
XENIA, OHIO

BROWNIES

1 cup shortening

1 (1-oz.) square semisweet chocolate

2$\frac{1}{2}$ cups sugar

4 eggs, beaten

2 tablespoons almond-flavored liqueur

1$\frac{1}{2}$ cups all-purpose flour

$\frac{1}{2}$ teaspoon salt

FROSTING

$\frac{1}{4}$ cup butter

1 (1-oz.) square semisweet chocolate

2 tablespoons half-and-half

2 cups sugar

$\frac{1}{4}$ teaspoon salt

2 tablespoons almond-flavored liqueur

3 to 4 tablespoons sliced almonds

1 Heat oven to 400°F. Spray 8-inch square pan with nonstick cooking spray.

2 In heavy saucepan, melt shortening and 1 oz. chocolate over low heat, stirring constantly. Add 2$\frac{1}{2}$ cups sugar, stirring until combined. Remove from heat. Stir in eggs and 2 tablespoons of the almond-flavored liqueur.

3 In small bowl, combine flour and $\frac{1}{2}$ teaspoon salt; add to chocolate mixture, stirring well. Pour mixture into pan. Bake 20 minutes or until golden brown. Cool completely.

4 In medium saucepan, melt butter and 1 oz. chocolate over low heat. Stir in half-and-half. Add 2 cups sugar, $\frac{1}{4}$ teaspoon salt and 2 tablespoons almond-flavored liqueur. Stir until smooth. Spread mixture over cooled brownies. Sprinkle with almonds.

32 brownies

ALAN'S FAVORITE PUMPKIN BARS

JAYNE HORNSLER
CINCINNATI, OHIO

BARS

2 eggs

$\frac{1}{2}$ cup sugar

$\frac{1}{2}$ cup packed brown sugar

$\frac{1}{2}$ cup vegetable oil

1 cup canned pumpkin

1 cup all-purpose flour

$\frac{1}{2}$ teaspoon baking soda

$\frac{1}{2}$ teaspoon salt

1 teaspoon cinnamon

$\frac{1}{2}$ teaspoon ground ginger

$\frac{1}{2}$ teaspoon nutmeg

FROSTING

1 (3-oz.) pkg. cream cheese

$\frac{1}{4}$ cup butter, softened

1 cup powdered sugar

1 teaspoon vanilla

1 Heat oven to 350°F. Spray 15$\frac{1}{2}$x10$\frac{1}{2}$x1-inch baking pan with nonstick cooking spray.

2 In medium bowl, beat eggs, sugar, brown sugar and oil at medium speed until blended. Add pumpkin; beat well.

3 In separate bowl, combine flour, baking soda, salt, cinnamon, ginger and nutmeg; mix well. Add flour mixture to pumpkin mixture; mix well. Pour into pan. Bake 25 minutes or until lightly browned; cool in pan.

4 To prepare frosting, beat cream cheese and butter in another medium bowl. Add remaining 1 cup powdered sugar and vanilla; beat until smooth. Spread mixture thinly over pumpkin bars. Store in refrigerator.

4 dozen bars

CHOCOLATE REFRESHERS

JOYCE QUICK
CANDOR, NEW YORK

BARS

1$\frac{1}{4}$ cups all-purpose flour

$\frac{3}{4}$ teaspoon baking soda

$\frac{1}{2}$ teaspoon salt

1$\frac{1}{4}$ cups chopped dates

$\frac{3}{4}$ cup packed brown sugar

$\frac{1}{2}$ cup butter

$\frac{1}{2}$ cup water

1 cup semisweet chocolate chips (6 oz.)

2 eggs

$\frac{1}{2}$ cup orange juice

$\frac{1}{2}$ cup milk

1 cup chopped nuts

FROSTING

1$\frac{1}{2}$ cups powdered sugar

2 tablespoons butter

2 teaspoons grated orange peel

2 to 3 tablespoons orange juice

1 Heat oven to 350°F. Spray 15$\frac{1}{2}$x10$\frac{1}{2}$x1-inch baking pan with nonstick cooking spray.

2 In medium bowl, combine flour, baking soda and salt; set aside. In large saucepan, combine dates, brown sugar, $\frac{1}{2}$ cup butter and water. Cook, stirring constantly, until dates soften. Stir in chips. Beat in eggs at medium speed. Add flour mixture alternately with $\frac{1}{2}$ cup orange juice and milk; blend thoroughly. Stir in nuts. Spread mixture into pan.

3 Bake 25 to 30 minutes or until golden brown. Cool completely.

4 To prepare frosting, in medium bowl, combine powdered sugar, 2 tablespoons butter, orange peel and 2 to 3 tablespoons orange juice; mix until well blended and smooth. Spread over bars. Store in refrigerator.

3 dozen bars

PEANUT BUTTER CRUNCH BARS

NANCY OLTMAN
HASTINGS, NEBRASKA

$\frac{1}{2}$ cup butter

1 cup chunky peanut butter

2 cups packed brown sugar

3 eggs

2 cups all-purpose flour

1$\frac{1}{2}$ teaspoons baking soda

3 cups old-fashioned or quick-cooking oats

2 cups semisweet chocolate chips (12 oz.)

1 (14-oz.) can sweetened condensed milk

2 cups peanut butter chips (12 oz.)

1 cup crispy rice cereal

1 Heat oven to 350°F. Spray 15$\frac{1}{2}$x10$\frac{1}{2}$x1-inch baking pan with nonstick cooking spray.

2 In large bowl, beat butter and peanut butter at medium speed until well combined. Add brown sugar and continue beating until light and fluffy. Add eggs one at time, beating well after each addition. Add flour and baking soda. Beat in oats. Press mixture into pan.

3 Bake 20 minutes. Remove from oven; sprinkle with chocolate chips. Let stand 5 minutes or until chips are almost melted. With spatula, spread melted chips evenly over crust. Refrigerate 30 minutes or until chocolate layer is set.

4 In microwave-safe bowl, combine milk and peanut butter chips. Microwave on High 1 minute; stir. Continue to microwave until chips are almost melted. Stir to finish melting. Stir in cereal; pour over bars. Spread evenly with spatula. (Peanut butter chip layer will marble slightly with chocolate.) Let bars set 30 minutes.

5 dozen bars

CREME DE MENTHE BROWNIES WITH A CRUST

CREME DE MENTHE BROWNIES WITH A CRUST

SUSAN BETTINGER
BATTLE CREEK, MICHIGAN

BROWNIES

1 cup sugar

$1/2$ cup butter

4 eggs

2 cups chocolate syrup

1 teaspoon vanilla

1 cup all-purpose flour

$1/2$ teaspoon salt

FROSTING

2 cups powdered sugar

3 tablespoons crème de menthe syrup*

$1/2$ cup butter

TOPPING

1 cup semisweet chocolate chips (6 oz.)

$1^1/3$ cups butter

1 Heat oven to 350°F. Spray 13x9-inch pan with nonstick cooking spray.

2 In large bowl, beat 1 cup sugar and $1/2$ cup butter. Beat in eggs, chocolate syrup and vanilla. Stir in flour and salt; mix until well blended. Pour into pan. Bake 30 minutes or just until brownies start to pull away from sides of pan. Cool on wire rack.

3 In large bowl, combine 2 cups sugar, crème de menthe syrup and $1/2$ cup butter; mix until smooth. Spread frosting over cooled brownies.

4 In small saucepan, heat chocolate chips and $1^1/3$ cups butter over medium-high heat until melted. Remove from heat; cool. Pour chocolate topping over frosting. Let stand until chocolate is set. Cut into 2-inch squares or triangles.

TIP *Crème de menthe syrup can be found in the ice cream section of most grocery stores.

About 3 dozen brownies

BROWNIE ICE CREAM CONES

MARY STRONG
PLEASANTON, TEXAS

1 (4-oz.) bar German sweet chocolate

$1/4$ cup butter

$3/4$ cup sugar

2 eggs

$1/2$ cup all-purpose flour

$1/2$ cup chopped walnuts

1 teaspoon vanilla

24 flat-bottomed ice cream cones

24 scoops ice cream

Chocolate sprinkles

1 In large microwave-safe bowl, microwave chocolate and butter on High, stirring occasionally, until melted. Remove from microwave; cool. Add sugar and eggs; mix well. Stir in flour, walnuts and vanilla.

2 Heat oven to 350°F. Meanwhile, place cones in muffin cups. Fill each cone half full of chocolate mixture. Bake 20 to 22 minutes or until toothpick inserted in center comes out almost clean. Top each cone with scoop of ice cream; top with sprinkles.

2 dozen cones

CREAMY PUDDINGS, CUSTARDS,

MOUSSES & MERINGUES

RICE PUDDING WITH RASPBERRY SAUCE (page 94)

STRAWBERRY PEACH PARFAITS

PAM MILLIGAN
ARROYO GRANDE, CALIFORNIA

3 ripe peaches, peeled, sliced

2 cups strawberries, sliced

2 tablespoons sugar

1/3 cup apple cider

3 egg yolks

3/4 cup powdered sugar

1/2 teaspoon nutmeg

1 cup heavy cream

Whipped Cream

1 In large bowl, blend together fruit, sugar and 1 tablespoon of the cider.

2 In small saucepan, combine egg yolks, powdered sugar and nutmeg. Add remaining cider. Cook over medium-low heat, stirring constantly, 10 minutes or until thickened. Cool. Beat cream at high speed until soft peaks form; fold into egg mixture.

3 In parfait glasses, layer fruit and cream mixture ending with fruit layer. Garnish with dollop of whipped cream. Store in refrigerator.

4 servings

FRENCH BANANA ECLAIR

KITTI BOESEL
GLEN BURNIE, MARYLAND

PASTRY

1 cup water

1/2 cup butter

1/2 teaspoon salt

1 cup all-purpose flour

4 eggs

FILLING AND ICING

2 cups heavy cream

2 tablespoons sugar

2 ripe large bananas, mashed

1/4 cup crème de cacao

1 cup powdered sugar

1/3 cup unsweetened cocoa

1 tablespoon melted butter

1 teaspoon vanilla

3 to 4 tablespoons boiling water

1 Heat oven to 400°F. Spray baking sheet with non-stick cooking spray.

2 To prepare dough, bring 1 cup water, 1/2 cup butter and salt to a boil in medium saucepan over medium heat. Add 1 cup flour, stir vigorously with spoon until dough forms ball and leaves sides of pan. Remove from heat. Beat in eggs, one at a time, continuing to beat until dough is stiff and glossy. Reserve one-third of the dough.

3 On baking sheet, form dough into rectangle about 2 inches wide. Spoon reserved dough into mounds on top of rectangle. Bake 30 minutes. Remove from oven; make slits along sides of èclair about 2 inches apart to allow steam to escape. Bake an additional 10 minutes; remove to wire rack.

4 Slice off top. Remove any soft dough inside. Cool completely.

5 To prepare filling, beat cream in large bowl at medium speed. Add 2 tablespoons sugar; whip until stiff peaks form. Fold bananas into whipped cream with crème de cacao. Fill èclair with cream mixture. Replace top. Stir together 1 cup sugar, cocoa, 1 tablespoon butter and vanilla to form a smooth icing. Add boiling water as needed to smooth icing. Pour icing over èclair. Store in refrigerator.

9 servings

PAVLOVA

GWENETH M. CLAUSON
EL CAJON, CALIFORNIA

6 egg whites

1/8 teaspoon salt

2 cups superfine sugar

1 1/2 teaspoons white vinegar

1/2 teaspoon vanilla

1 (8-oz.) container frozen whipped topping, thawed

Fresh fruit

1 Heat oven to 300°F.

2 In large bowl, beat egg whites and salt at medium speed until stiff peaks form; add sugar slowly until completely dissolved. Stir in vinegar and vanilla. Mixture should be stiff enough to hold its shape, but not dry.

3 Make 9-inch circle with egg white mixture, building 1-inch rim around outside of circle. Bake 45 minutes. Turn oven off. Leave in oven 1 1/2 hours. Remove from oven and cool completely.

4 Remove circle to serving plate; fill center with whipped topping and fruit. Serve immediately. Store in refrigerator.

8 servings

CHEESE FLAN

MICHAEL DENIKE
BREVARD, NORTH CAROLINA

1/2 cup sugar

1 (14-oz.) can sweetened condensed milk

2 cups water

6 eggs

1 (8-oz.) pkg. cream cheese

1 teaspoon vanilla

1 Heat oven to 350°F.

2 Caramelize sugar in ring mold or 8-inch square pan; set aside.

3 Combine milk and water together in small saucepan. In blender, combine eggs, cream cheese, vanilla and milk mixture; blend well. Pour mixture into mold. Place mold in water bath. Bake 90 minutes or until firm. Let flan cool before inverting onto serving dish. Store in refrigerator.

8 servings

CHOCOLATE VELVET MARSHMALLOW PUDDING

GWEN CAMPBELL
STERLING, VIRGINIA

1 cup bread cubes

2 tablespoons melted butter

1 egg

1/4 cup sugar

1/4 teaspoon salt

1/2 teaspoon vanilla

1/4 teaspoon cinnamon

2 cups milk

1/2 cup raisins

3 tablespoons unsweetened cocoa

1 cup heavy cream, whipped

1/2 cup snipped large marshmallows

1 Heat oven to 350°F. Spray 8-inch square pan with nonstick cooking spray.

2 In large bowl, combine bread cubes, butter, egg, sugar, salt, vanilla, cinnamon, milk, raisins and cocoa; mix thoroughly. Pour mixture into pan set in 9-inch pan of water. Bake 1 hour or until set; cool. Serve with whipped cream combined with marshmallows. Store in refrigerator.

4 servings

CHOCOLATE TULIP CUPS

CHOCOLATE TULIP CUPS

DEBBIE DOUGELA
ROSWELL, GEORGIA

1 (1-lb. 4-oz.) pkg. chocolate almond bark *

18 (11-inch) balloons, blown to 5 inches in diameter, tied

1 In large saucepan over low heat, melt chocolate, stirring constantly. When chocolate is melted, cool at least 20 minutes, stirring frequently.

2 Place one sheet of parchment paper on flat work surface. For each tulip cup, very carefully place balloon in chocolate. In slow movement, roll balloon forward, then backward, then to the left then right. This forms a tulip shaped cup. Make sure there is enough coverage so that chocolate is at least $1/8$ inch thick and even. Carefully lift balloon out of chocolate; place tied side up on parchment paper. Allow chocolate to harden about 40 minutes.

3 Once hardened, carefully pop balloon with pin; the balloon should peel out easily, leaving a chocolate cup to fill with desired fillings (chocolate mousse, fruit, mousse, ice cream, pudding, etc.).

TIP *It is important to cool chocolate before dipping balloons. If chocolate is too hot, it will be difficult to remove balloons from chocolate cups.

18 servings

CARAMEL APPLE PUDDINGS

MICHELLE HALL
CHESTER SPRINGS, PENNSYLVANIA

CUSTARD

3 eggs

$1/3$ cup sugar

$1 1/2$ cups milk

1 teaspoon vanilla

CARAMEL SAUCE

3 cups sugar

$1/2$ cup water

$1/8$ teaspoon cream of tartar

2 cups heavy cream

$3/4$ cup melted butter

6 cups toasted bread cubes

$1 1/2$ cups sautèed apple slices

1 In large bowl, whisk eggs. Add $1/3$ cup sugar; mix until well combined. Add milk and vanilla; mix thoroughly. Strain through fine mesh strainer.

2 Mix 3 cups sugar, water and cream of tartar in medium saucepan. Wash down sides with brush. Boil without stirring until amber color. In medium bowl, combine cream and butter.

3 Heat oven to 350°F.

4 In 6-oz. custard or soufflé cups, layer toasted bread cubes, apples and custard mixture. Place cups in large roasting pan; add about 1 inch boiling water to pan. Place pan in oven; bake 50 to 60 minutes or until toothpick inserted in center comes out clean. Serve warm with ice cream, if desired. Store in refrigerator.

12 servings

DATE-BUTTERSCOTCH TRIFLE

FANNIE KLINE
MILLERSBURG, OHIO

CAKE

2 cups boiling water

2 teaspoons baking soda

2 tablespoons butter

2 cups chopped dates

2 eggs, lightly beaten

2 teaspoons vanilla

1/2 teaspoon salt

2 cups sugar

2 cups all-purpose flour

SAUCE

1 cup packed brown sugar

3 tablespoons all-purpose flour

1/8 teaspoon salt

1 cup boiling water

3 tablespoons butter

1/2 teaspoon vanilla

TOPPING

3 cups heavy cream

3/4 cup powdered sugar

1 tablespoon vanilla

2 bananas, sliced

1 cup chopped walnuts

1 Heat oven to 350°F. Spray 13x9-inch pan with nonstick cooking spray.

2 In small heatproof bowl, pour 2 cups boiling water, baking soda and 2 tablespoons butter over dates; cool. In large bowl, combine eggs, 2 teaspoons vanilla, 1/2 teaspoon salt, sugar and 2 cups flour; mix well. Add date mixture; stir until well combined. Pour mixture into pan.

3 Bake 25 to 30 minutes or until golden brown; cool. Cut into 1-inch cubes. (Cake can be prepared 2 days ahead.)

4 To prepare sauce, combine brown sugar, 3 tablespoons flour and 1/8 teaspoon salt in small saucepan. Add 1 cup boiling water; cook 5 minutes or until thickened, stirring constantly. Stir in 3 tablespoons butter and 1/2 teaspoon vanilla; cool.

5 To prepare topping, beat cream at medium-high speed in large bowl. Add 3/4 cup powdered sugar and 1 tablespoon vanilla.

6 Layer pudding cake cubes in bottom of trifle bowl. Add layers of whipped cream, bananas, nuts and dollop of butterscotch sauce.

7 Repeat layers twice. Garnish with butterscotch drizzle and nuts, if desired. Let stand 1 to 2 hours in cool place. Store in refrigerator.

10 to 12 servings

STRAWBERRY CUSTARD

PAMELA DAVIS
EGG HARBOR, WISCONSIN

2 cups milk

4 eggs

1/2 cup honey

1 teaspoon vanilla

1/4 teaspoon nutmeg

2 cups fresh strawberries, sliced

1 Heat oven to 350°F. In large bowl, beat milk, eggs, honey, vanilla and nutmeg at medium speed until blended. Pour mixture into 6 (8-oz.) custard cups or 1 (6-cup) baking dish. Divide strawberries among cups.

2 Place custard cups or baking dish in pan of hot water; bake 30 to 40 minutes or until custard is firm and toothpick inserted in center comes out clean. The strawberries will rise to top of custard during baking. Store in refrigerator.

6 servings

BLUEBERRY BREAD PUDDING

SARAH ROARK
ROSSVILLE, ILLINOIS

1 1/4 cups scalded milk

1/4 cup honey

1/2 teaspoon salt

1/2 teaspoon vanilla

1/2 teaspoon lemon extract

2 eggs, beaten

2 cups bread cubes

1 cup blueberries

1 Heat oven to 350°F. Spray 2-quart casserole with nonstick cooking spray.

2 In large bowl, combine milk, honey, salt, vanilla, lemon extract, eggs, bread cubes and blueberries; mix lightly. Pour mixture into casserole. Bake about 25 minutes or until golden brown. Serve warm or cold with cream or sauce. Store in refrigerator.

10 to 12 servings

YESTERYEAR'S BANANA-RICE PUDDING

GWEN CAMPBELL
STERLING, VIRGINIA

PUDDING

1/2 cup long-grain rice

2 cups boiling water

1 1/2 cups milk

1/4 cup sugar

1/4 teaspoon salt

2 egg yolks

1 tablespoon butter

1 teaspoon vanilla

1 teaspoon rum

2 bananas, sliced

MERINGUE

2 egg whites

1 tablespoon sugar

1 teaspoon cream of tartar

1 teaspoon rum

1 Heat oven to 325°F.

2 Place rice in saucepan with boiling water; boil 15 minutes, stirring occasionally. Drain and rinse under cold running water. In medium saucepan, combine milk, rice, 1/4 cup sugar and salt. Cook, covered, over low heat until rice is tender.

3 In small bowl, beat egg yolks; add 2 heaping tablespoons of hot rice mixture to eggs. Pour egg mixture back into rice mixture; cook, stirring constantly, 1 minute. Remove from heat. Add butter, vanilla and 1 teaspoon rum; mix well. Place rice in 11x7-inch pan; top rice with sliced bananas across.

4 To prepare meringue, beat egg whites in large bowl at medium-low speed until frothy. Gradually add 1 tablespoon sugar, cream of tartar and 1 teaspoon rum; beating at medium speed until stiff peaks form. Spread mixture carefully over bananas. Bake 30 minutes or until meringue is golden-tipped. Store in refrigerator.

8 to 10 servings

COCONUT CREME BRULEE WITH CARAMELIZED GINGER SUGAR

LINDA FISHER
WATERLOO, IOWA

1 cup heavy cream

1 cup unsweetened coconut milk

1 vanilla bean, split

1/8 teaspoon salt

4 egg yolks

1/2 cup sugar

1 tablespoon dark rum

Ginger sugar*

1 Heat oven to 300°F. In medium saucepan, combine cream, coconut milk, vanilla bean and salt. Heat very slowly until surface begins to shimmer.

2 While cream mixture is heating, place egg yolks, sugar and rum in large bowl; whisk to blend. Remove cream from heat. Add cream gradually to egg mixture to prevent curdling, whisking gently to avoid air bubbles.

3 Strain custard into large glass measuring cup and pour into 4 (1/2-cup) ramekins, filling to rim. Place ramekins in roasting pan; pour in enough water to reach halfway up sides of ramekins. Cover loosely with aluminum foil. Bake 1 1/4 hours or until custard is firm around edges.

4 Remove ramekins from water bath and let cool. Cover and refrigerate ramekins at least 4 hours or overnight.

5 Heat broiler. Sprinkle tops with thin coating of ginger sugar. Place under broiler to caramelize sugar. Let cool; serve immediately. Store in refrigerator.

TIP *To make ginger sugar, peel a small knob of fresh ginger. Place in a resealable plastic food-storage bag or glass container along with 1/2 cup sugar. Mix well. Refrigerate up to one week.

4 servings

SPANISH-STYLE CREAM CHEESE CUSTARDS

BERNADETTE MEJIA
HUNTSVILLE, GEORGIA

2 cups sugar

2 (8-oz.) pkg. cream cheese, softened

2 cups heavy cream

4 eggs

2 teaspoons vanilla

1 Heat oven to 350°F.

2 Heat 1 cup of the sugar in medium saucepan over medium-low heat. Once sugar begins to melt, stir constantly until caramelized. Immediately pour into 8 (6-oz.) custard cups, coating bottoms and sides. Set aside.

3 In large bowl, beat cream cheese with 2 cups cream at high speed until smooth. Slowly add remaining 1 cup sugar, eggs and vanilla; beat at medium speed until well blended.

4 Pour mixture into cooled custard cups; place in large roasting pan. Add water to pan half way up sides of cups. Bake 50 to 60 minutes or until golden brown and set. (Custards will rise, but will fall after cooling.) Cool and refrigerate; serve chilled. Store in refrigerator.

8 servings

RICE PUDDING WITH RASPBERRY SAUCE

VIVIAN NIKANOW
CHICAGO, ILLINOIS

PUDDING

2/3 cup sugar

1/2 cup water

2 (1/4-oz.) pkg. unflavored gelatin

1/2 teaspoon salt

2 cups milk

1 1/2 cups cooked white rice

2 teaspoons vanilla

1 cup heavy cream

RASPBERRY SAUCE

1 (10-oz.) pkg. frozen raspberries, thawed

1 tablespoon cold water

2 teaspoons cornstarch

1 Heat sugar, 1/2 cup water, gelatin and salt in large saucepan, stirring constantly until gelatin dissolves, about 1 minute. Stir in milk, rice and vanilla. Place saucepan in bowl of ice water, stirring occasionally 10 minutes or until mixture mounds slightly when dropped from spoon.

2 In large chilled bowl, beat cream at high speed until stiff peaks form. Fold cream into rice mixture. Pour into 6-cup mold or serving bowl. Cover and refrigerate 3 hours or until firm.

3 Unmold by dipping briefly in warm water and loosening edges with spatula; invert onto serving plate.

4 To prepare raspberry sauce, press raspberries through sieve to remove seeds; reserve syrup. In small saucepan, heat sieved raspberries with syrup to a boil. In small bowl, mix 1 tablespoon water and cornstarch; stir into raspberries. Heat to boiling, stirring constantly. Boil and stir 1 minute; cool. Spoon sauce over pudding. Store in refrigerator.

8 servings

RICE PUDDING WITH
RASPBERRY SAUCE

CREME BRULEE NOUVEAU

GAIL LONGSTRETH
HONOLULU, HAWAII

2 cups heavy cream

4 egg yolks

1/2 cup sugar

1 tablespoon vanilla

3/4 teaspoon powdered sugar

1 Heat oven to 350°F.

2 Heat cream over low heat until bubbles form around edge of pan; remove from heat. In medium bowl, beat egg yolks and sugar at medium speed until thick, about 3 minutes. Gradually beat warm cream into egg yolks. Stir in vanilla; pour into 6 (6-oz.) ramekins.

3 Place ramekins in baking pan filled with 1/2 inch warm water. Bake about 45 minutes or until set. Remove ramekins from water; refrigerate several hours or overnight.

4 Heat broiler. Sprinkle each custard evenly with powdered sugar. Place ramekins on baking sheet. Broil until sugar topping is golden brown. Place immediately in refrigerator; cool thoroughly at least 1 hour before serving. Decorate with one-half of strawberry on top, if desired. Store in refrigerator.

6 servings

CHOCOLATE CREAM PUFF RING

CHRISTINA MORREL
YELLVILLE, ARKANSAS

PASTRY	FILLING AND GLAZE
1/2 cup butter	2 cups semisweet chocolate chips (12 oz.)
1/2 teaspoon salt	1/4 cup plus 1 1/2 teaspoons milk
1 cup water	3 tablespoons butter
1 cup all-purpose flour	2 large eggs
4 eggs	2 cups heavy cream
	1 1/2 teaspoons light corn syrup
	1 pint strawberries

1 To prepare pastry, heat 1/2 cup butter, salt and water in large saucepan over medium heat until butter melts and mixture boils. Remove from heat. With wooden spoon, vigorously stir in flour. Add 4 eggs to flour mixture, one at a time, beating well after each addition, until mixture is smooth.

2 Heat oven to 400°F. Lightly spray baking sheet with nonstick cooking spray; lightly flour. Using 7-inch plate as a guide, trace circle in flour on baking sheet. Drop batter by heaping tablespoons into 12 mounds, inside circle, to form ring. With moistened finger, smooth tops. Bake 40 minutes or until golden. Turn off oven; let ring stand in oven for 15 minutes. Remove ring from oven, cool on baking sheet on wire rack. Meanwhile, prepare filling.

3 To prepare filling, heat 1 1/2 cups of the chocolate chips, 1/4 cup of the milk and 2 tablespoons of the butter in large saucepan over low heat, stirring occasionally, until smooth. Add 2 eggs one at a time, stirring constantly with wire whisk. Continue whisking chocolate mixture an additional 5 minutes until slightly thickened. Transfer to bowl; cover surface with plastic wrap. Refrigerate 30 minutes.

4 In large bowl, beat cream at medium speed until stiff peaks form. With rubber spatula, fold whipped cream into cooled chocolate mixture, one-half at a time, until blended. With long serrated knife, cut cooled ring horizontally in half. Spoon chocolate mousse filling into bottom of ring. Replace top of ring. Refrigerate until ready to serve.

5 To prepare glaze, heat remaining 1/2 cup chocolate chips, remaining 1 tablespoon butter, remaining 1 1/2 teaspoons milk and corn syrup in medium saucepan over low heat, stirring constantly, until smooth. Spoon over ring. Fill center of ring with strawberries. Store in refrigerator.

12 servings

KIWI CLOUD

SONJA CISNA
PEORIA, ILLINOIS

5 kiwi fruit, peeled, cut into chunks

1/2 cup sugar

2 teaspoons cornstarch

1 tablespoon water

1 (8-oz.) container frozen whipped topping, thawed

1 Puree kiwi in food processor or blender.

2 In small saucepan, whisk together 1/2 cup of the kiwi puree, sugar, cornstarch and water. Simmer over medium heat, stirring constantly, 4 to 5 minutes or until mixture thickens. Remove from heat; transfer to medium bowl. Cool. Stir in remaining kiwi puree; refrigerate until chilled.

3 Gently fold whipped topping into chilled kiwi mixture. Spoon into individual serving dishes; refrigerate about 3 hours or until set. Garnish with kiwi slices, if desired. Store in refrigerator.

4 servings

LESLIE'S LEMON SNOW

LESLIE STEVENS
LOS ANGELES, CALIFORNIA

1 cup sugar

1/4 teaspoon salt

1/4 cup all-purpose flour

6 tablespoons fat-free cholesterol-free egg product

1/4 cup lemon juice

1 1/2 cups nonfat milk

1 tablespoon grated lemon peel

3 egg whites

1 Heat oven to 325°F. Spray 8-inch square pan with nonstick cooking spray.

2 In large bowl, blend together sugar, salt and flour. In medium bowl, beat egg product at high speed until light and fluffy. Stir in lemon juice, milk and lemon peel. Stir egg mixture into flour mixture just until blended. Fold in egg whites.

3 Pour into pan. Set baking pan in larger pan of hot water. Bake about 40 minutes or until toothpick inserted in center comes out clean. Serve warm. Store in refrigerator.

8 servings

MAPLE BREAD PUDDING

VIVIAN NIKANOW
CHICAGO, ILLINOIS

BREAD PUDDING

12 (1-inch-thick) slices French bread or 5 cups cubed bread

3 eggs

2 1/2 cups milk

1/3 cup pure maple syrup

1/4 cup packed brown sugar

3 tablespoons melted butter

1 teaspoon vanilla

1/2 teaspoon ground cinnamon

1/8 teaspoon nutmeg

SAUCE

1/4 cup water

2 teaspoons cornstarch

2 tablespoons butter

1/2 cup pure maple syrup

2 tablespoons sliced almonds, toasted

1 Heat oven to 350°F. Place bread in 8-inch square pan.

2 In medium bowl, beat eggs at medium speed until frothy. Add milk, 1/3 cup syrup, brown sugar, 3 tablespoons butter, vanilla, cinnamon and nutmeg; mix well. Pour egg mixture over bread. Bake 50 minutes or until toothpick inserted in center comes out clean. Set aside.

3 To prepare sauce, combine water and cornstarch in small bowl; mix well. In small saucepan, melt 2 tablespoons butter. Add 1/2 cup syrup and cornstarch mixture; cook until slightly thickened. Remove from heat; stir in almonds. Spread over bread pudding. Store in refrigerator.

8 to 10 servings

ESPRESSO BREAD PUDDING WITH
ALMOND-FLAVORED LIQUEUR CUSTARD SAUCE

ESPRESSO BREAD PUDDING WITH ALMOND-FLAVORED LIQUEUR CUSTARD SAUCE

CHRISTOPHER FOGERTY
GREENTOWN, INDIANA

BREAD PUDDING

6 eggs, separated

1¼ cups sugar

1 tablespoon vanilla

2 cups heavy cream

¼ cup unsalted butter

2 tablespoons coarsely ground espresso beans

1 cup semisweet chocolate chips (6 oz.)

1 lb. bakery-style* cinnamon doughnuts, broken into 1-inch pieces

SAUCE

10 egg yolks

1 cup sugar

3 cups whole milk

3 tablespoons almond-flavored liqueur

2 teaspoons vanilla

1 Heat oven to 325°F. Spray 12 (6-oz.) custard cups with nonstick cooking spray; set aside.

2 Separate eggs into 2 medium bowls. Into egg yolks, whisk ¾ cup of the sugar and 1 tablespoon vanilla; set aside.

3 In medium saucepan, combine cream, butter and espresso powder. Bring mixture to a simmer over medium-high heat, stirring frequently. Strain mixture through fine mesh strainer and return to pan over medium heat until hot. Gradually pour espresso mixture into yolk mixture, whisking constantly. Stir in chocolate chips until melted and smooth.

4 Beat egg whites at medium speed until soft peaks form; slowly add remaining ½ cup sugar; beat until stiff but not dry. Fold into chocolate mixture. Add doughnuts; toss to coat evenly. Fill custard cups with pudding mixture; let stand 1 hour.

5 Place custard cups in large roasting pan with 1 to 2 inches water in bottom. Bake 50 to 60 minutes or until toothpick inserted in center comes out clean. Invert puddings onto individual plates.

6 To prepare sauce, whisk egg yolks and 1 cup sugar in large bowl until well blended. In medium saucepan, bring milk to a simmer over medium heat. Whisk hot milk slowly into egg mixture. Return to saucepan over low heat, stirring constantly. Cook 8 to 12 minutes or until mixture just coats back of metal spoon. Strain custard through fine mesh strainer into medium bowl; whisk in liqueur and 2 teaspoons vanilla. Cool to room temperature; refrigerate 3 hours. Serve with bread pudding. Store in refrigerator.

TIP *Use yeast-raised doughnuts.

12 servings

STRAWBERRY AND CARAMELIZED BANANA TRIFLE

VICKI BENSINGER
ST. LOUIS, MISSOURI

CUSTARD

3/4 cup sugar

2 tablespoons all-purpose flour

2 tablespoons cornstarch

2 cups milk

6 egg yolks

6 tablespoons butter

1 teaspoon vanilla

CARAMEL SYRUP

1 cup sugar

1/3 cup plus 5 tablespoons water

FILLING

1 (10-oz.) baked pound cake

2/3 cup seedless raspberry jam

8 tablespoons dark rum

2 lb. fresh strawberries, hulled, sliced

8 medium bananas, peeled, cut into 1/3-inch-thick slices

Sliced strawberries

Sliced bananas

TOPPING

1 1/2 cups heavy cream

3 tablespoons powdered sugar

1/2 teaspoon vanilla

1 To prepare custard, combine 3/4 cup sugar, flour and cornstarch in small saucepan. Whisk in milk gradually; cook until thickened, stirring constantly. In small bowl, beat egg yolks lightly. Stir one-half cup of the hot mixture into the egg yolks; stir egg yolks into the hot mixture. Cook until thickened, stirring constantly. Remove from heat. Stir in butter and 1 teaspoon vanilla.

2 Place one piece of plastic wrap directly on the surface of custard; let stand until cool or place in refrigerator until ready to use. Custard can be prepared 1 day ahead.

3 To prepare syrup, stir 1 cup sugar and 1/3 cup of the water in small saucepan over low heat until sugar dissolves. Increase heat. Bring to a boil without stirring until syrup turns a deep amber color. Brush down sides of pan with wet pastry brush; swirl pan occasionally. Remove from heat. Add 3 tablespoons of the water (mixture will bubble vigorously). Stir until caramel is smooth. Pour caramel into medium bowl. Mix in remaining 2 tablespoons water, cool. Caramel can be prepared 1 day ahead. Cover and let stand at room temperature.

4 Cut cake into 1-inch cubes. Split cubes in half; spread jam on one side of cube. Reassemble cake cubes with jam in center. Arrange one-half of the cake cubes to cover bottom of 3 1/2- to 4-quart trifle dish. Brush cake layer with 2 tablespoons of the rum. Top with one-half of sliced berries, arranging some to show at sides of dish. Add banana slices to caramel syrup; gently stir to coat. Using a slotted spoon, remove banana slices, a few at a time, draining all excess caramel back into bowl. Layer one-half of banana slices on top of berries, arranging some to show at sides of dish. Spoon one-half of custard over bananas, spreading to side of dish. Repeat layering with cake, rum, berries, banana slices and custard. Arrange remaining cake cubes on top of custard; press gently to compact. Brush with remaining 2 tablespoons rum. Cover trifle. Refrigerate at least 4 hours and up to 10 hours. Cover remaining caramel syrup; store at room temperature.

5 Slice additional bananas. Arrange fruit on top of trifle, leaving 1-inch plain border at edge. Brush fruit with enough caramel syrup to glaze.

6 In medium bowl, combine cream, 3 tablespoons powdered sugar and 1/2 teaspoon vanilla; beat until soft peaks form. Spoon into pastry bag and pipe around edges of fruit or spread over trifle or around fruit. Store in refrigerator.

20 servings

DELICIA DE AMEIXA
(THREE-LAYER PRUNE DELIGHT)

STEPHANIE FISHER-MATHEWS
SARASOTA, FLORIDA

CAKE

1 (12-oz.) box pitted prunes

2 cups water

2 tablespoons sugar

4 egg whites

ENGLISH CREAM

1 tablespoon cornstarch

1 tablespoon milk

1 1/2 cups whole milk

4 egg yolks

2 tablespoons sugar

1 teaspoon vanilla

2 tablespoons white wine

TOPPING

1 cup heavy cream

1 tablespoon powdered sugar

1 Heat oven to 350°F. Spray 9-inch pie pan with nonstick cooking spray.

2 Using greased kitchen shears, cut each prune into 3 pieces.

3 In small saucepan, combine prunes, water and 2 tablespoons sugar. Bring to a boil over medium heat; simmer until syrup thickens. In large bowl, beat egg whites at medium speed until stiff peaks form. Fold egg whites into prune mixture. Spread into pan. Bake 15 minutes.

4 In small bowl, dissolve cornstarch in 1 tablespoon milk. Combine 1 1/2 cups milk, egg yolks, 2 tablespoons sugar, 1 teaspoon vanilla and white wine in medium saucepan. Stir in cornstarch mixture. Stirring constantly, heat until thickened over low heat. Spread over baked prune layer.

5 In large bowl, beat cream and 1 tablespoon powdered sugar at medium speed until soft peaks form.

6 Spread topping over English Cream layer. Refrigerate 2 to 3 hours or until cold and firm. Garnish with toasted almonds or candied violets, if desired. Cut into wedges or squares. Store in refrigerator.

8 servings

FUDGE BATTER PUDDING

SONJA CISNA
PEORIA, ILLINOIS

2 tablespoons melted butter

1 cup sugar

1 teaspoon vanilla

1 cup all-purpose flour

1/2 cup unsweetened cocoa

1 teaspoon baking powder

3/4 teaspoon salt

1/2 cup milk

1/2 cup chopped nuts

1 2/3 cups boiling water

1 Heat oven to 350°F. Spray 8-inch square pan with nonstick cooking spray.

2 In large bowl, mix butter, 1/2 cup of the sugar and vanilla. In another bowl, combine flour, 3 tablespoons of the cocoa, baking powder and 1/2 teaspoon of the salt. Add alternately with milk to butter mixture; mix well. Stir in nuts.

3 In small bowl, mix together remaining 1/2 cup sugar, 5 tablespoons cocoa, 1/4 teaspoon salt and boiling water. Pour into pan. Drop batter by tablespoons onto hot mixture. Bake 40 to 45 minutes or until toothpick inserted in center comes out clean. Serve warm. Store in refrigerator.

9 servings

ZABAGLIONE
(ITALIAN CUSTARD)

DANIELA RAGUSA BALL
SALEM, OREGON

6 egg yolks

1/2 cup sugar

1/2 cup sweet Marsala wine

In small saucepan, combine egg yolks, sugar and wine over very low heat. Beating constantly with wire whisk, cook about 10 minutes or until mixture is very fluffy. Serve in dessert bowls while still warm, or spoon over fresh raspberries or strawberries. Store in refrigerator.

2 1/2 cups

CAKES

CHERRY BLUSH CAKE
WITH SABAYON (page 120)

GRAMMA JEAN'S BANANA CAKE

CLAUDIA WENDEL
FRESNO, CALIFORNIA

1/2 cup shortening

1 1/2 cups sugar

2 eggs, well beaten

2 1/4 cups all-purpose flour

1/2 teaspoon baking powder

1/4 teaspoon baking soda

1/2 teaspoon salt

1 teaspoon vinegar

1/4 cup milk

1 cup mashed banana

1 teaspoon vanilla

1 cup heavy cream, whipped, sweetened

2 bananas, sliced, sprinkled with lemon juice

1 Heat oven to 350°F. Spray 2 (8- or 9-inch) round cake pans with nonstick cooking spray.

2 In medium bowl, beat shortening at medium-high speed until fluffy. Slowly add sugar and eggs; beat well. In another bowl, combine flour, baking powder, baking soda and salt. Stir in vinegar and milk.

3 Alternately add sugar mixture, flour mixture and mashed banana to shortening mixture. Beat in vanilla; pour evenly into pans.

4 Bake 40 to 45 minutes or until cake springs back when touched. Turn cake out onto wire rack; cool thoroughly. Frost with sweetened whipped cream; garnish with banana slices. Store in refrigerator.

8 to 10 servings

TROPICAL CARROT CAKE

EVA RIOS
AUSTIN, TEXAS

CAKE

2 cups all-purpose flour

2 teaspoons baking powder

1 teaspoon each baking soda, cinnamon

1/2 teaspoon each salt, nutmeg, allspice

4 large eggs

2 cups sugar

1 1/4 cups canola oil

2 cups grated raw carrot

1 (8 1/2-oz.) can crushed pineapple, drained, juice reserved

1 cup chopped pecans

1/2 cup flaked coconut

FROSTING

4 oz. cream cheese, softened

6 tablespoons butter, softened

4 cups powdered sugar

1 to 1 1/2 tablespoons reserved pineapple juice

1 cup flaked coconut

1 Heat oven to 350°F. Spray 3 (9-inch) round cake pans with nonstick cooking spray.

2 In large bowl, mix together flour, baking powder, baking soda, cinnamon, salt, nutmeg and allspice; set aside. In large bowl, beat eggs at low speed 30 seconds. Increase speed to medium; beat in sugar. Stir in oil, flour mixture, carrot and pineapple. Mix well. Stir in pecans and 1/2 cup coconut. Spread cake batter evenly among 3 pans.

3 Bake 40 to 45 minutes or until cake springs back when touched. Cool cakes in pans 10 minutes; turn out onto cooling racks and cool completely.

4 To prepare frosting, beat cream cheese and butter at medium speed in large bowl until fluffy; beat in powdered sugar. Add pineapple juice, 1 teaspoon at a time, until frosting is smooth.

5 Place first layer on cake plate top-side-down; frost with frosting. Place second cake layer top-side-down on first layer; frost. Place third layer with top-side-up up; frost top and sides. Sprinkle remaining 1 cup coconut over cake and on sides, pressing gently. Sprinkle finely gated pecans over top, if desired. Store in refrigerator.

12 servings

DECADENT DOUBLE-CHOCOLATE LAYER CAKE

DAVID A. HEPPNER
BRANDON, FLORIDA

CAKE

1/2 cup finely chopped semisweet chocolate (3 oz.)

1 1/2 cups hot coffee

3 cups sugar

2 1/2 cups all-purpose flour

1 1/2 cups unsweetened cocoa

2 teaspoons baking soda

3/4 teaspoon baking powder

1 1/4 teaspoons salt

3 large eggs

3/4 cup vegetable oil

1 1/2 cups buttermilk

3/4 teaspoon vanilla

FROSTING

1 (1-lb.) block semisweet chocolate

1 cup heavy cream, whipped

2 tablespoons sugar

2 tablespoons light corn syrup

1/4 cup unsalted butter

1 Heat oven to 300°F. Line 3 (9-inch) round cake pans with parchment paper; spray paper with non-stick cooking spray.

2 In large bowl, combine 1/2 cup chocolate with coffee. Let mixture stand, stirring occasionally, until chocolate is melted and mixture is smooth.

3 In another large bowl, mix 3 cups sugar, flour, cocoa, baking soda, baking powder and salt. In another bowl, beat eggs on high speed about 3 minutes or until thickened slightly and lemon-colored. Slowly add oil, buttermilk, vanilla and melted chocolate mixture to eggs, beating until well combined. Add sugar mixture; beat at high speed just until combined. Divide batter evenly among cake pans.

4 Bake 50 to 60 minutes or until toothpick inserted in center comes out clean. Cool layers completely in pans. Run a thin knife around edges of pans; invert onto racks. Carefully remove parchment paper.

5 To prepare frosting, finely chop 1 lb. chocolate. In medium saucepan, bring cream, 2 tablespoons sugar and corn syrup to a boil over low heat, whisking until sugar is dissolved. Remove pan from heat; add chocolate, whisking until chocolate is melted. Cut butter into pieces and add to frosting; whisk until smooth.

6 Transfer frosting to bowl; cool. Stir occasionally until smooth. Spread between cake layers and over top and sides. Refrigerate cake up to 3 days; bring cake to room temperature before serving. Store in refrigerator.

12 to 16 servings

CHOCOHOLICS BROWNIE TORTE

GWEN CAMPBELL
STERLING, VIRGINIA

TORTE

1/2 cup unsalted butter

1/2 cup light corn syrup

1 cup semisweet chocolate chips (6 oz.)

1/2 cup sugar

3 eggs

1 tablespoon unsweetened cocoa

1 teaspoon vanilla

1 cup all-purpose flour

1 cup chopped walnuts

GLAZE

1/2 cup semisweet chocolate chips (3 oz.)

2 tablespoons butter

1 tablespoon light corn syrup

1/2 teaspoon almond extract

1/2 cup drained chopped Maraschino cherries

1 Heat oven to 350°F.

2 In medium saucepan over low heat, combine 1/2 cup butter and 1/2 cup syrup. Heat until melted; stir in 1 cup chocolate chips until melted. Add sugar, eggs and cocoa. Stir until well blended. Stir in vanilla, flour and nuts. Pour mixture into 9-inch round cake pan.

3 Bake 30 minutes. Invert cake onto wire rack to cool.

4 To prepare glaze, melt 1/2 cup chocolate chips and 2 tablespoons butter with 1 tablespoon syrup in small saucepan over low heat; remove from heat. Add almond extract and cherries; mix well. Spread over torte, allowing glaze to cascade down sides of cake.

12 servings

PINEAPPLE POUND CAKE

CATHY LEATHERWOOD
DALLAS, TEXAS

CAKE

1/2 cup vegetable shortening

1 cup butter

2 3/4 cups sugar

6 eggs

3 cups all-purpose flour

1 teaspoon baking powder

1/4 cup milk

1 teaspoon vanilla

1 (8-oz.) can crushed pineapple

GLAZE

1 1/2 cups powdered sugar

1 cup drained crushed pineapple

1/4 cup butter

1 Heat oven to 325°F. Spray 10-inch tube pan with nonstick cooking spray.

2 In large bowl, beat shortening, 1 cup butter and sugar at high speed until fluffy; add eggs one at a time, beating well after each addition. Combine flour and baking powder; add gradually, alternating with milk. Add vanilla. Stir in undrained pineapple. Pour into pan; place in cold oven.

3 Bake 90 minutes. Let cake stand in pan 5 minutes.

4 Meanwhile, prepare glaze. In another large bowl, combine powdered sugar, drained pineapple and 1/4 cup butter; mix well. Run knife around edge to loosen cake; invert onto serving plate. While cake is still hot, spoon glaze over top.

16 servings

CREAM OF COCONUT CAKE

DIANA DANIEL
DALLAS, TEXAS

CAKE

1 (18.5-oz.) box white cake mix

1 cup sour cream

3/4 cup vegetable oil

4 eggs

1 (3-oz.) can cream of coconut

ICING

10 tablespoons butter, softened

1 (8-oz.) pkg. plus 1 (3-oz.) pkg. cream cheese

1 1/2 teaspoons vanilla

5 cups powdered sugar

1/2 cup grated coconut, if desired

1 Heat oven to 325°F. Spray 3 (8-inch) round cake pans with nonstick cooking spray.

2 In large bowl, combine cake mix, sour cream, oil, eggs and cream of coconut. Beat 2 minutes at medium speed. Pour mixture evenly into prepared pans.

3 Bake 25 to 30 minutes or until toothpick inserted in center comes out clean. Cool 10 minutes in pan; remove. Let cool completely on wire rack.

4 To prepare icing, beat butter, cream cheese and vanilla in another large bowl at medium speed until smooth. Gradually beat in powdered sugar until frosting is smooth. Stir in coconut. Spread over cake. Store in refrigerator.

8 servings

HUMMINGBIRD CAKE

KITTI BOESEL
GLEN BURNIE, MARYLAND

CAKE

3 cups all-purpose flour

2 cups sugar

1 teaspoon baking soda

1 teaspoon salt

1 1/2 teaspoons cinnamon

1 1/2 cups vegetable oil

3 eggs

1 1/2 teaspoons vanilla

1 (8-oz.) can crushed pineapple

2 cups chopped bananas

1 cup raisins, nuts or coconut

FROSTING

1 (8-oz.) pkg. cream cheese, softened

1/2 cup butter, softened

2 teaspoons vanilla

1 (16-oz.) pkg. powdered sugar

1 Heat oven to 350°F. Spray 10-inch tube pan with nonstick cooking spray.

2 In large bowl, combine flour, sugar, baking soda, salt and cinnamon. Set aside. In another large bowl, stir together vegetable oil, eggs, 1 1/2 teaspoons vanilla, pineapple, bananas and raisins with spoon. Stir in flour mixture with spoon. Pour into pan.

3 Bake 60 to 70 minutes or until toothpick inserted in center comes out clean. Cool in pan or on wire rack 10 minutes.

4 To prepare frosting, beat cream cheese, butter, 2 teaspoons vanilla and powdered sugar in large bowl at medium speed until smooth. Spread frosting over cake. Store in refrigerator.

8 servings

DOUBLE CHOCOLATE FUDGE CAKE

DOUBLE CHOCOLATE FUDGE CAKE

AMY SMOUSE
CORTEZ, COLORADO

CAKE

2$\frac{1}{4}$ cups semisweet chocolate chips (14 oz.)

2 cups butter

1$\frac{1}{2}$ cups sugar

1 cup half-and-half

1 tablespoon vanilla

$\frac{1}{2}$ teaspoon salt

8 eggs

GLAZE

2 tablespoons butter

1 cup semisweet chocolate (6 oz.)

3 tablespoons milk

2 tablespoons white corn syrup

1 cup heavy cream

GARNISH

1 cup heavy cream

1 cup assorted raspberries, blackberries

1 Heat oven to 350°F. Spray 9-inch round cake pan with nonstick cooking spray.

2 Combine 2$\frac{1}{4}$ cups chocolate chips, 2 cups butter, sugar, half-and-half, vanilla and salt in medium saucepan over medium-low heat. Cook, stirring frequently, 2 minutes or until chocolate is melted. Remove from heat. In large bowl, beat eggs until well blended; stir chocolate mixture into eggs. Pour into prepared pan.

3 Bake 45 minutes; cool completely on wire rack. Wrap in plastic wrap; refrigerate 6 hours.

4 Remove cake from pan. To prepare glaze, melt 2 tablespoons butter and 1 cup chocolate chips in medium saucepan over low heat; remove from heat. Beat in milk and corn syrup. Spread warm glaze over top and sides of cake. In medium bowl, beat cream at high speed until soft peaks form. Garnish cake with whipped cream and berries.

24 servings

GRAHAM-CRACKER CAKE

MARY J. EDGAR
CINCINNATI, OHIO

CAKE

$\frac{1}{2}$ cup butter

1 cup sugar

3 eggs, separated

1 teaspoon vanilla

3 cups crushed graham crackers

6 tablespoons all-purpose flour

1$\frac{1}{2}$ teaspoons baking powder

$\frac{1}{8}$ teaspoon nutmeg

$\frac{3}{4}$ cup milk

$\frac{1}{4}$ teaspoon cinnamon

$\frac{1}{2}$ cup chopped walnuts

ICING

$\frac{1}{2}$ cup butter

1 (8-oz.) pkg. cream cheese

1 (16-oz.) pkg. powdered sugar

2 teaspoons vanilla

8 walnut halves

1 Heat oven to 350°F. Spray 2 (8-inch) round cake pans with nonstick cooking spray.

2 In large bowl, beat $\frac{1}{2}$ cup butter and sugar at high speed until fluffy. Beat in egg yolks and 1 teaspoon vanilla. Combine graham cracker crumbs, flour, baking powder, cinnamon and nutmeg; add alternately with milk to butter mixture.

3 In another large bowl, beat egg whites at high speed until stiff peaks form. Fold egg whites into batter. Pour into pans.

4 Bake 25 to 30 minutes or until toothpick inserted in center comes out clean. Cool in pans 5 minutes; remove from pans and cool on wire rack.

5 To prepare frosting, beat $\frac{1}{2}$ cup butter and cream cheese at high speed in medium bowl until fluffy. Add powdered sugar and 2 teaspoons vanilla; beat until light and fluffy. Spread frosting over cakes. Garnish with walnuts. Store in refrigerator.

8 servings

PRALINE CHOCOLATE CAKE

MARLENE HEINLE
GARLAND, TEXAS

CAKE

1/2 cup butter

1/4 cup heavy cream

1 cup packed brown sugar

3/4 cup coarsely chopped pecans

1 (18.5-oz.) box devils food cake mix

TOPPING

1 3/4 cups heavy cream

1/4 cup powdered sugar

1/4 teaspoon vanilla

Whole pecans

1 Heat oven to 325°F. Spray 2 (9-inch) round cake pans with nonstick cooking spray.

2 In heavy saucepan over medium-low heat, heat butter, 1/4 cup heavy cream, brown sugar and pecans until butter and brown sugar are melted; pour mixture into pans. Set aside.

3 Prepare cake mix according to package directions. Pour batter over pecan mixture; bake 35 to 40 minutes or until toothpick inserted in center comes out clean. Cool 5 minutes. Remove from pans; cool on wire racks.

4 To prepare topping, beat 1 3/4 cups cream, powdered sugar and vanilla in chilled medium bowl until stiff peaks form.

5 Place 1 layer on serving plate; spread one-half of topping over cake. Place second layer cake on topping; frost. Arrange whole pecans around top of cake. Store in refrigerator.

16 servings

CHOCOLATE VIENNA TORTE

BARBARA BRANDEL
LAKELAND, FLORIDA

TORTE

6 eggs, separated

1 cup sugar

3/4 cup all-purpose flour

1 teaspoon each salt, baking powder, vanilla

1/2 teaspoon cream of tartar

3/4 cup grated semisweet chocolate

FROSTING

2 cups heavy cream

5 tablespoons powdered sugar

1 teaspoon vanilla

Grated semisweet chocolate

1 Heat oven to 350°F. Line 2 (9-inch) round cake pans with parchment paper; spray paper with nonstick cooking spray. (Do not spray sides of pan.)

2 In large bowl, beat egg yolks at high speed until thick and lemon-colored. Gradually add 1/2 cup of the sugar; continue to beat 5 to 10 minutes. Set aside.

3 In medium bowl, combine flour, salt and baking powder. Set aside. In another large bowl, beat egg whites and cream of tartar at medium-low speed until foamy. Increase speed to medium; gradually add remaining 1/2 cup sugar and continue beating until whites are very stiff. Sprinkle 1 teaspoon vanilla over egg whites. Sprinkle ¾ cup grated chocolate over egg whites; fold a few times. (Chocolate will not be fully incorporated.)

4 Quickly stir flour mixture into yolk mixture; fold into egg whites until fully blended. Divide batter evenly between pans. Bake 30 minutes. Remove pans from oven; remove cake from pans immediately. Remove parchment paper. Cool on wire racks.

5 To prepare frosting, combine cream, powdered sugar and 1 teaspoon vanilla in large bowl; beat until stiff peaks form. Spread on cake. Sprinkle chocolate over cake and refrigerate several hours before serving. Store in refrigerator.

12 to 14 servings

CHOCOLATE DREAM

SHERAMIE HENDRY
LAKEWOOD, WASHINGTON

CAKE

2 eggs

$1\frac{1}{3}$ cups sugar

$1\frac{1}{4}$ cups all-purpose flour

$\frac{1}{4}$ cup unsweetened cocoa

$1\frac{1}{2}$ teaspoons baking soda

$\frac{1}{4}$ teaspoon salt

$\frac{2}{3}$ cup vegetable oil

1 cup buttermilk

1 teaspoon vanilla

FILLING

1 (3.4-oz.) pkg. instant vanilla pudding mix

$2\frac{3}{4}$ cups milk

FROSTING

1 cup heavy cream

$\frac{1}{3}$ cup unsweetened cocoa

$\frac{1}{2}$ cup powdered sugar

1 teaspoon vanilla

1 Heat oven to 350°F. Spray 2 (9-inch) round cake pans with nonstick cooking spray.

2 In small bowl, beat eggs and $1\frac{1}{3}$ cups sugar at high speed until thick and light colored. In large bowl, mix flour, $\frac{1}{4}$ cup cocoa, baking soda and salt. Add oil, buttermilk and 1 teaspoon vanilla to flour mixture; beat until well blended. Fold in egg mixture; blend well. Pour evenly into pans.

3 Bake 30 minutes. Cool in pans 10 minutes; remove from pans and cool on wire rack.

4 To prepare filling, combine pudding mix and milk in large bowl; mix well. Refrigerate.

5 To prepare frosting, combine cream, $\frac{1}{3}$ cup cocoa, powdered sugar and 1 teaspoon vanilla in another large bowl; beat at medium speed until fluffy. Refrigerate.

6 Spread pudding mixture on one cake layer; top with other layer. Frost only top of cake with whipped cream mixture. Refrigerate 2 hours. Store in refrigerator.

16 servings

CINNAMON SWIRL POUND CAKE

VIVIAN NIKANOW
CHICAGO, ILLINOIS

$2\frac{1}{4}$ cups sugar

2 tablespoons cinnamon

3 cups all-purpose flour

3 teaspoons baking powder

$\frac{1}{2}$ teaspoon salt

1 cup butter

1 cup milk

4 eggs

1 teaspoon vanilla

1 Heat oven to 350°F. Spray 10-inch tube pan with nonstick cooking spray.

2 In small bowl, combine $\frac{1}{4}$ cup of the sugar and cinnamon; set aside. In another bowl, sift flour, baking powder and salt; set aside. In large bowl, beat butter and remaining 2 cups sugar at medium speed until light and fluffy.

3 In small bowl, combine milk, eggs and vanilla. Add milk mixture and flour alternately to butter mixture. Pour one-half of the batter into pan; sprinkle with one-half the cinnamon mixture. Add remaining one-half batter; top with remaining one-half cinnamon mixture.

4 Bake 1 hour. Cool thoroughly in pan on wire rack.

16 servings

JO'S PECAN RUM CAKE

PEGGY WINKWORTH
DURANGO, COLORADO

CAKE

3/4 cup finely chopped pecans

1 (18.5-oz.) box butter-recipe yellow cake mix

1 (3.4-oz.) pkg. instant vanilla pudding mix

4 eggs

1/2 cup light rum

1/2 cup vegetable oil

1/2 cup water

1/2 cup butter

GLAZE

1/2 cup butter

1/2 cup rum

1 cup sugar

1/4 cup water

1 Heat oven to 325°F. Spray 12-cup Bundt pan with nonstick cooking spray.

2 Sprinkle pecans in bottom of pan. In large bowl, combine cake mix, pudding mix, eggs, 1/2 cup rum, oil, 1/2 cup water and 1/2 cup butter; beat at medium speed about 3 minutes or until smooth. Pour into pan.

3 Bake 50 to 60 minutes or until toothpick inserted in center comes out clean. Cool 20 minutes in pans. With thin spatula, loosen edges and center of cake. Invert cake onto serving plate. Poke holes in cake with long-tined fork or bamboo skewer.

4 To prepare glaze, in small saucepan, boil butter, 1/2 cup rum, 1 cup sugar and 1/4 cup water 3 minutes. Drizzle glaze over cake. Cover cake with aluminum foil and refrigerate up to 3 days.

16 servings

LEMON-CREAM CHEESE POUND CAKE

PEGGY YAMAGUCHI-LAZAR
EUGENE, OREGON

CAKE

3 cups sugar

1 1/4 cups butter, softened

1 (8-oz.) pkg. cream cheese, softened

3 tablespoons lemon juice

2 teaspoons vanilla

1 teaspoon lemon extract

1/2 teaspoon orange extract

1/8 teaspoon salt

6 eggs

2 3/4 cups all-purpose flour

GLAZE

1 cup powdered sugar

1 tablespoon butter

2 teaspoons grated lemon peel

2 tablespoons lemon juice

1 Heat oven to 325°F. Spray 10-inch tube pan or 12-cup Bundt pan with nonstick cooking spray; lightly flour.

2 In large bowl, beat sugar, 1 1/4 cups butter and cream cheese at high speed until fluffy. Beat in lemon juice, vanilla, lemon extract, orange extract and salt. Add eggs one at a time, beating after each addition. Add flour; beat until smooth. Spread in pan.

3 Bake 1 hour or until golden brown and toothpick inserted in center comes out clean. Cool 10 minutes; remove from pan. Cool completely on wire rack.

4 To prepare glaze, mix powdered sugar, 1 tablespoon butter, lemon peel and 2 tablespoons lemon juice in another large bowl. Add additional lemon juice, 1 teaspoon at a time, until smooth. Spread glaze over cake, allowing some to drizzle down side.

16 servings

LEMON-CREAM CHEESE POUND CAKE

SWEET POTATO POUND CAKE

CAROL HAWLEY
FREDERICK, MARYLAND

CAKE

1 cup butter, softened

2 cups sugar

2½ cups mashed cooked sweet potatoes

4 eggs

3 cups all-purpose flour

¼ teaspoon salt

2 teaspoons baking powder

1 teaspoon baking soda

½ teaspoon nutmeg

1 teaspoon cinnamon

1 teaspoon vanilla

GLAZE

2 to 3 tablespoons orange juice

1 cup powdered sugar

1 Heat oven to 350°F. Spray 10-inch tube pan with nonstick cooking spray.

2 In large bowl, beat butter and sugar at high speed until fluffy. Add potatoes; beat until light and fluffy. Add eggs separately, beating well after each addition. Combine flour, salt, baking powder, baking soda, nutmeg and cinnamon; add to butter mixture slowly. Add vanilla; beat well. Pour mixture into pan.

3 Bake 90 minutes or until toothpick inserted in center comes out clean. Cool 30 minutes in pan.

4 Stir 2 tablespoons orange juice into powdered sugar. If necessary, add more orange juice, 1 teaspoon at a time, until drizzling consistency. Drizzle over warm cake.

16 servings

DELUXE OLD-FASHIONED CHOCOLATE CHOCOLATE-CHIP CAKE

WITH CHOCOLATE FUDGE FROSTING

LIZ LARSEN
VALLEY VILLAGE, CALIFORNIA

CAKE

3 oz. cup unsweetened chocolate

1⅓ cups water

¾ cup butter

2¼ cups packed brown sugar

2 eggs

1 teaspoon vanilla

2 cups all-purpose flour

1 teaspoon baking soda

½ teaspoon salt

2 cups semisweet chocolate chips (12 oz.)

FROSTING

2 cups semisweet chocolate chips (12 oz.)

¼ cup shortening

3 cups powdered sugar

½ cup milk

1 Heat oven to 350°F. Spray 2 (8-inch) round cake pans with nonstick cooking spray.

2 Place unsweetened chocolate in small saucepan with ⅓ cup of the water. Stir constantly over low heat until chocolate is melted. Remove from heat; cool. In large bowl, beat butter and brown sugar at high speed until light and fluffy. Add eggs and vanilla; beat well. Beat in chocolate. In medium bowl, combine flour, baking soda and salt. Add alternately with remaining 1 cup water, beating at medium speed until well blended; fold in 2 cups chocolate chips. Combine butter and flour mixtures; pour batter evenly into pans.

3 Bake 35 to 40 minutes or until toothpick inserted in center comes our clean. Cool completely on wire racks.

4 To prepare frosting, melt 2 cups chocolate chips with shortening in small saucepan. Stir in powdered sugar and milk; remove from heat. Stir mixture with spoon until smooth. Spread frosting over cake.

8 to 10 servings

PUMPKIN-GINGER CAKE

VIVIAN NIKANOW
CHICAGO, ILLINOIS

CAKE

3 cups all-purpose flour

2 teaspoons baking powder

2 teaspoons baking soda

1 tablespoon pumpkin pie spice

1 teaspoon ground ginger

1 cup butter, softened

1 cup packed brown sugar

4 eggs

1/4 cup molasses

1 teaspoon vanilla

1 (16-oz.) can pumpkin (not pumpkin pie filling)

1/2 cup sour cream

1/2 cup chopped walnuts

1/4 cup minced crystallized ginger

ICING

3/4 teaspoon ground ginger

1 cup powdered sugar

1 tablespoon plus 1 teaspoon water

1 Heat oven to 350°F. Spray 12-cup Bundt pan with nonstick cooking spray.

2 In medium bowl, combine flour, baking powder, baking soda, pumpkin pie spice and 1 teaspoon ground ginger; set aside. In large bowl, combine butter, brown sugar, eggs, molasses, vanilla and pumpkin; beat at medium speed until well combined. Beat in flour mixture alternately with sour cream. Stir in walnuts and crystallized ginger. Pour batter into pan.

3 Bake 50 to 55 minutes or until toothpick inserted in center comes out clean. Cool in pan on wire rack 10 minutes. Remove from pan; cool completely.

4 To prepare icing, combine 3/4 teaspoon ground ginger, powdered sugar and water in small bowl. Stir until well combined. Drizzle over cake.

16 servings

GLAZED BUNDT CAKE WITH BERRIES

KAREN BALLANCE
WOLF LAKE, ILLINOIS

CAKE

1 1/4 cups butter

2 1/2 cups sugar

7 eggs

2 1/2 teaspoons vanilla

2 1/2 cups all-purpose flour

GLAZE

2 to 3 teaspoons water

2 cups powdered sugar

1/4 teaspoon vanilla

Fresh berries

1 Heat oven to 325°F. Spray 12-cup Bundt pan with nonstick cooking spray; lightly flour.

2 In large bowl, beat butter at low speed until light and fluffy. Slowly add sugar. Add eggs one at a time, beating well after each addition. Add 2 1/2 teaspoons vanilla; mix well. Add flour slowly; beat well. Pour mixture into pan.

3 Bake 1 hour. Cool cake in pan 10 minutes. Remove from pan.

4 To prepare sauce, in medium bowl, add water to powdered sugar, 1 teaspoon at a time, until thin enough to drizzle. Stir in 1/4 teaspoon vanilla. Pour glaze over warm cake.

16 servings

APPLE CAKE

APPLE CAKE

RITA HASHEMI
DUBLIN, OHIO

3/4 cup butter

1 3/4 cups sugar

1/2 cup water

3/4 teaspoon cinnamon

2 Granny Smith apples, peeled, thinly sliced

3 egg yolks

2 eggs

2 tablespoons brandy

2 teaspoons vanilla

1 cup all-purpose flour

1 teaspoon baking powder

1 Heat oven to 350°F. Spray 9-inch round cake pan with nonstick cooking spray; lightly dust with sugar, tapping out excess.

2 In large saucepan, combine 1/4 cup of the butter, 3/4 cup of the sugar, water and cinnamon; bring to a boil. Reduce heat and simmer 5 minutes. Arrange apples decoratively in bottom of pan; top with syrup.

3 In large bowl, beat together remaining 1/2 cup butter and 1 cup sugar until smooth. Beat in egg yolks, eggs, brandy and vanilla until well blended. Fold in flour and baking powder. Spoon batter over apples.

4 Bake 35 to 40 minutes. Remove from oven; cool 3 minutes. Loosen edges of cake; invert onto serving platter. Serve warm.

8 servings

I'LL-START-MY-DIET-NEXT-WEEK CUPCAKES

DIANNA HOWARD
COOS BAY, OREGON

CAKE

3 cups all-purpose flour

2 cups sugar

1/2 cup unsweetened cocoa

2 teaspoons baking soda

1 teaspoon salt

2/3 cup vegetable oil

2 cups water

2 tablespoons vinegar

2 teaspoons vanilla

FILLING

1 (8-oz.) pkg. cream cheese, softened

1 egg

1/3 cup sugar

1/4 teaspoon salt

1 cup semisweet chocolate chips (6 oz.)

1 Heat oven to 350°F. Line 24 muffin cups with paper liners.

2 In large bowl, combine flour, 2 cups sugar, cocoa, baking soda and 1 teaspoon salt; set aside. In another large bowl, combine oil, water, vinegar and vanilla. Slowly combine flour mixture and oil mixture until smooth. Fill muffin cups two-thirds full.

3 To prepare filling, beat cream cheese, egg, 1/3 cup sugar and 1/4 teaspoon salt in another large bowl at medium speed until fluffy. Stir in chocolate chips. Drop heaping teaspoonful onto each cupcake.

4 Bake 25 minutes. Remove from pan; cool on wire rack. Store in refrigerator.

2 dozen cupcakes

COFFEE-BANANA CAKE

VIVIAN NIKANOW
CHICAGO, ILLINOIS

1 cup butter, softened

1½ cups sugar

3½ cups all-purpose flour

1 tablespoon baking powder

1 teaspoon baking soda

¼ teaspoon salt

1 cup mashed ripe bananas

½ cup coffee-flavored liqueur

4 eggs

¼ cup milk

1 teaspoon vanilla

¾ cup flaked coconut

¾ cup chopped walnuts

1 Heat oven to 350°F. Spray 10-inch tube pan with nonstick cooking spray.

2 In large bowl, beat butter and sugar at medium speed until fluffy. Beat in flour, baking powder, baking soda, salt, bananas, coffee-flavored liqueur, eggs, milk and vanilla; mix thoroughly. Stir in coconuts and walnuts. Pour mixture into pan.

3 Bake 45 to 50 minutes or until golden brown. Remove from oven and let stand 10 minutes in pan. Invert onto wire rack; cool completely. Dust with powdered sugar, if desired.

9 servings

COCONUT-ORANGE CHIFFON CAKE

E. M. (BETTE) BANJACK
NORRISTOWN, PENNSYLVANIA

CAKE

2 cups all-purpose flour

1½ cups sugar

3 teaspoons baking powder

1 teaspoon salt

8 eggs, separated

1 teaspoon cream of tartar

½ cup vegetable oil

2 teaspoons vanilla

1 teaspoon grated lemon peel

¾ cup water

ICING

4 tablespoons butter

2 cups powdered sugar

Dash salt

1 teaspoon vanilla

3 tablespoons milk

1 cup flaked coconut

2 to 3 tablespoons grated orange peel

1 Heat oven to 325°F.

2 In medium bowl, combine flour, sugar, baking powder and salt; set aside.

3 In large bowl, beat egg whites at medium-high speed until stiff peaks form. Add cream of tartar. In another large bowl, beat together oil, egg yolks, 2 teaspoons vanilla, lemon peel and water at medium speed until blended. Stir flour mixture and oil mixture together. Fold in egg whites just enough to blend ingredients together. Pour into ungreased 10-inch tube pan.

4 Bake 50 minutes or until cake springs back when touched, increasing heat to 350°F during last 10 minutes.

5 To prepare icing, beat butter and powdered sugar in medium bowl at medium speed until fluffy. Add salt and 1 teaspoon vanilla. Beat in milk slowly until icing is smooth. Frost cake with icing; sprinkle with coconut and orange peel.

12 servings

CHOCOLATE MINT CAKE

BARBARA BRANDEL
LAKELAND, FLORIDA

4 eggs, separated

1 (18.5-oz.) box yellow cake mix

1 (3.4-oz.) pkg. instant pistachio pudding mix

1/2 cup orange juice

1/2 cup water

1/2 cup vegetable oil

1/2 cup crème de menthe liqueur

1 teaspoon vanilla

1/2 cup plus 2 tablespoons chocolate syrup

1 Heat oven to 350°F. Spray 12-cup Bundt pan with nonstick cooking spray; lightly flour.

2 In large bowl, beat egg whites at medium-low speed until frothy. Increase speed to medium-high and beat until stiff peaks form. Set aside. In another large bowl, combine cake mix, pudding mix, orange juice, water, oil, liqueur and vanilla; mix well. Fold in egg whites. This will create a green batter.

3 Pour 2/3 batter into prepared pan. Mix chocolate syrup with remaining 1/3 batter in bowl. Pour over batter. Do not mix.

4 Bake 1 hour or until toothpick inserted in center comes out clean. Cool 10 minutes in pan. Invert onto wire rack; cool completely. Dust cake with powdered sugar or drizzle with chocolate sauce, if desired.

16 servings

POTICA CAKE

SMELIA DAMJANOVICH
ST. PETERSBURG, FLORIDA

NUT MIXTURE

2 cups ground walnuts

1 1/2 cups packed brown sugar

2 tablespoons flour

1 1/2 teaspoons vanilla

1 teaspoon cinnamon

CAKE

3/4 cup butter

1 1/2 cups sugar

4 eggs

3 cups all-purpose flour

1 1/2 teaspoons baking powder

1 1/2 teaspoons baking soda

1 1/2 teaspoons vanilla

2 cups sour cream

1 Heat oven to 350°F.

2 In large bowl, combine walnuts, brown sugar, 2 tablespoons flour, 1 1/2 teaspoons vanilla and cinnamon; mix thoroughly.

3 Set aside. In another large bowl, beat butter and sugar at medium speed until fluffy. Add eggs one at a time, beating well after each addition. Combine 3 cups flour, baking powder and baking soda in another large bowl; add slowly to butter mixture. Stir 1 1/2 teaspoons vanilla into sour cream; mix well. Stir into batter. Swirl in butter mixture. Do not mix. Pour into ungreased 12-inch tube pan.

4 Bake 1 1/4 hours or until toothpick inserted in center comes out clean. Cool cake in pan 15 to 30 minutes or until slightly warm. Remove cake from pan. Sift powdered sugar over cake, if desired. Store in refrigerator.

8 servings

THE ULTIMATE FLOURLESS CHOCOLATE CAKE

BRENDA JONES
LEXINGTON, SOUTH CAROLINA

1 (1-lb.) block semisweet chocolate

1/2 lb. unsalted butter, cut into chunks

1/4 cup strong coffee

8 large eggs, cold

1 Adjust oven rack to lower middle position; heat oven to 325°F. Line bottom of 8-inch springform pan with parchment paper; spray sides of pan with nonstick cooking spray. Wrap outside of pan with heavy-duty aluminum foil; place in large roasting pan.

2 Melt chocolate, butter and coffee in large heat-proof bowl over pan of barely simmering water until smooth and very warm, stirring occasionally. Or, heat in microwave-safe bowl at medium power 4 to 6 minutes, stirring occasionally. Meanwhile, in large bowl, beat eggs at high speed 5 minutes.

3 Fold in one-third of eggs into chocolate mixture using large rubber spatula only until mixed; fold in remaining egg mixture until mixture is homogenous.

4 Pour batter into pan; smooth surface with spatula. Set roasting pan on oven rack and pour enough boiling water to come about halfway up side of springform pan.

5 Bake 22 to 25 minutes or until cake has risen slightly, edges are just beginning to set and thin crust has formed on surface.

6 Remove cake from water bath; set on wire rack. Cool to room temperature. Cover and refrigerate overnight. About 30 minutes before serving, remove pan sides, invert cake onto sheet of parchment paper. Peel off paper; turn right-side-up on serving plate.

8 servings

CHERRY BLUSH CAKE WITH SABAYON

PAM MILLER
FALCON, COLORADO

CAKE

1/2 cup butter, softened

1/2 cup whipped cream cheese

3 cups sugar

6 eggs

4 1/2 cups all-purpose flour

1 teaspoon baking powder

2 teaspoons cherry extract

1/2 cup maraschino cherry juice

30 maraschino cherries, chopped, patted dry with paper towel

SABAYON SAUCE

8 egg yolks

2/3 cup sugar

1 cup dry sherry

1 cup heavy cream

Cherry brandy, if desired

Dark chocolate sauce

Chocolate-dipped cherries, if desired

1 Heat oven to 325°F. Spray 10-inch tube pan with nonstick cooking spray.

2 In large bowl, beat butter and cream cheese at high speed until blended. Slowly add 3 cups sugar; beat until light and fluffy. Add eggs one at a time, beating well after each addition. Combine 4 cups of the flour with baking powder; add to butter mixture and blend well. Stir in cherry extract and juice. Toss diced cherries in remaining 1/2 cup flour. Stir cherries and flour into batter; mix well. Pour batter into pan.

3 Bake 1 1/4 to 1 1/2 hours or until toothpick inserted in center comes out clean. Cool in pan 15 minutes. Remove from pan; invert cake onto wire rack. Cool completely.

4 To prepare sabayon sauce, fill large saucepan half full of water; simmer. In medium bowl, beat egg yolks and 2/3 cup sugar at medium speed 2 minutes. Mix in sherry. Place bowl over simmering water. (Do not allow bottom of bowl to touch water.) Beat until mixture doubles in volume and reaches 160°F on candy thermometer.

5 Pour into clean bowl; refrigerate about 1 hour or until cool. Beat cream until stiff peaks form; fold into sauce.

6 Arrange slices of cake on plate. Drizzle with cherry brandy. Drizzle with dark chocolate sauce. Garnish with chocolate-dipped cherries. Store in refrigerator.

16 servings

CHERRY BLUSH CAKE WITH SABAYON

CHERRY NUT CHIFFON CAKE

LINDA ALBERTS
SUN PRAIRIE, WISCONSIN

CAKE

2 cups all-purpose flour

1 1/2 cups sugar

1 tablespoon baking powder

1 teaspoon salt

1/2 cup vegetable oil

7 eggs, separated

1/2 cup water

1/4 cup maraschino cherry juice

1 teaspoon vanilla

1/2 teaspoon cream of tartar

1/2 cup finely chopped maraschino cherries, well drained

1/2 cup chopped nuts

ICING

3 1/2 cups powdered sugar

1/2 cup shortening

1/2 teaspoon salt

3 tablespoons maraschino cherry juice

3 tablespoons water

1 teaspoon lemon juice

1 Heat oven to 325°F.

2 In large bowl, combine flour, sugar, baking powder and 1 teaspoon salt. Make a well; add oil, egg yolks, 1/2 cup water, 1/4 cup cherry juice and vanilla. Beat at medium speed 1 minute or until smooth. In another large bowl, add cream of tartar to egg whites. Beat at medium speed until egg whites form stiff peaks. Pour egg yolk mixture gradually over beaten egg whites; gently fold with rubber spatula. Do not stir. Fold in cherries and nuts. Pour immediately into ungreased 10-inch tube pan.

3 Bake 55 minutes. Increase temperature to 350°F; bake an additional 10 to 15 minutes or until cake springs back when touched. Turn pan upside down over heatproof funnel until completely cooled. Loosen with spatula.

4 To prepare icing, beat powdered sugar with shortening and 1/2 teaspoon salt in large bowl at medium speed until blended. Stir in 3 tablespoons cherry juice, 3 tablespoons water and lemon juice; beat at medium speed until smooth. Cover tops and sides with icing.

8 servings

COFFEE-FLAVORED CAKE

ESTHER BUSEY
OKLAHOMA CITY, OKLAHOMA

1 (18.5-oz.) box devil's food cake mix

4 eggs

1 cup sour cream

1 cup coffee-flavored liqueur

1/2 cup melted butter

1 cup semisweet chocolate chips (6 oz.)

1 Heat oven to 350°F. Spray 12-cup Bundt pan with nonstick cooking spray; lightly flour.

2 In large bowl, combine cake mix, eggs, sour cream, liqueur and butter; beat at medium speed 3 to 5 minutes or until thoroughly blended. Stir in chocolate chips. Pour in pan.

3 Bake 50 to 60 minutes or until toothpick inserted near center comes out clean. Cool in pan 30 minutes. Remove from pan; invert onto wire rack. Cool completely.

16 servings

DATE PUDDING CAKE

LYNDA BURTON
HOUSTON, TEXAS

1 1/2 cups packed brown sugar

1 1/2 cups water

1 cup sugar

1 cup all-purpose flour

1 teaspoon baking powder

1/8 teaspoon salt

1/8 teaspoon salt

1 cup milk

1 teaspoon vanilla

1 cup chopped dates

1 cup chopped walnuts

1 Heat oven to 325°F. Combine brown sugar and water in medium saucepan; bring to a boil over high heat. Boil 5 minutes. Pour mixture into 3-quart casserole; cool.

2 In large bowl, combine sugar, flour, baking powder, salt, milk, vanilla, dates and walnuts; mix well. Pour over brown sugar layer.

3 Bake 35 to 40 minutes, increasing heat to 350°F during last 15 minutes of baking. Remove from oven; cool 5 minutes. Loosen cake with sharp knife. Invert cake onto serving platter.

16 servings

FRESH BERRY CAKE

DANIELA RAGUSA BALL
SALEM, OREGON

1 cup fresh strawberries

1 cup fresh blueberries

1 cup fresh raspberries

2 teaspoons grated lemon peel

1/2 cup sugar

1/2 cup orange-flavored liqueur or orange juice

1 (9 oz.) prepared angel food cake

1 In medium saucepan, cook berries, lemon peel, sugar and liqueur over medium-low heat until mixture begins to break down and bubble. Do not let mixture overcook; berries should remain whole. Set aside.

2 Cut cake into 2-inch pieces. Line cake pieces along bottom and sides of 3-quart casserole. Pour berry mixture into center of bowl; cover berry mixture completely with additional cake pieces.

3 Cover a heavy can with aluminum foil; place over top of cake. Refrigerate cake overnight. To serve, remove can and invert cake onto serving platter; decorate with additional berries, if desired. Store in refrigerator.

6 servings

PUMPKIN ROLL

PAM MILLIGAN
ARROYO GRANDE, CALIFORNIA

CAKE

3 eggs

1 cup sugar

2/3 cup pumpkin

1 teaspoon lemon juice

3/4 cup all-purpose flour

1 teaspoon baking powder

1/2 teaspoon salt

2 teaspoons cinnamon

1 teaspoon ground ginger

1/2 teaspoon nutmeg

1 cup chopped pecans

FILLING

1 cup powdered sugar

1/4 cup softened butter

1 (8-oz.) pkg. cream cheese, softened

1/2 teaspoon vanilla

2 tablespoons sweetened condensed milk

1 Heat oven to 350°F. Spray 15 1/2x10 1/2x1-inch baking pan with nonstick cooking spray. Line bottom of pan with parchment paper.

2 In medium bowl, beat eggs at high speed 5 minutes. Gradually add sugar, pumpkin and lemon juice. In separate bowl, mix flour, baking powder, salt, cinnamon, ginger and nutmeg; add to pumpkin mixture. Pour into pan. Sprinkle with pecans.

3 Bake 15 minutes or until toothpick inserted in center comes out clean.

4 Generously sift powdered sugar onto clean dish towel; invert cake onto towel. Carefully peel off parchment paper and lightly sift powdered sugar over cake. Roll up cake with towel from narrow end; let cool at least 30 minutes.

5 To prepare filling, beat powdered sugar, butter, cream cheese, vanilla and condensed milk in large bowl at medium speed until smooth. Unroll cake; spread with filling. Roll up again. Dust with powdered sugar. To serve, cut into 1-inch-thick slices. Store in refrigerator.

10 servings

CHEESECAKES & SPECIAL

OCCASION DESSERTS

CLAUDIA'S PUMPKIN-TOFFEE
CHEESECAKE (page 136)

RASPBERRY CHEESECAKE

VIVIAN NIKANOW
CHICAGO, ILLINOIS

1 cup graham-cracker crumbs

3 tablespoons sugar

¼ cup melted butter

1 (10-oz.) pkg. frozen raspberries, thawed

¼ cup cold water

1 (¼-oz.) pkg. unflavored gelatin

1 (8-oz.) pkg. cream cheese, softened

1 teaspoon vanilla

½ cup sugar

1 cup heavy cream, whipped

1 Heat oven to 350° F.

2 In large bowl, combine crumbs, 3 tablespoons sugar and butter; press into bottom of 9-inch springform pan. Bake 10 minutes; cool.

3 Drain raspberries; reserve juice. Set berries aside. In small saucepan, combine juice, cold water and gelatin. Let stand 5 minutes. Cook and stir over low heat until gelatin dissolves. Remove from heat; cool 10 minutes.

4 In large bowl, beat cream cheese, vanilla and ½ cup sugar at medium speed until blended. Add thawed berries and gelatin mixture; beat at low speed until thoroughly blended. Refrigerate 30 minutes or until partially set. (Be careful, as the mixture sets up quickly.) Gently fold in whipped cream. Spoon mixture into crust.

5 Refrigerate 6 hours or overnight. Run thin knife around edge of pan to loosen edges. Remove sides of pan. Top with fresh raspberries and whipped cream, if desired. Store in refrigerator.

10 servings

CHOCOLATE-GLAZED CHERRY CHEESECAKE

JOYCE QUICK
CANDOR, NEW YORK

10 to 12 cream-filled chocolate sandwich cookies, finely crushed (1 cup)

4 (8-oz.) pkg. cream cheese, softened

1¼ cups sugar

1 teaspoon vanilla

½ teaspoon almond extract

3 eggs

1 cup (10 oz.) Maraschino cherries, coarsely chopped

½ cup heavy cream, whipped

1 cup semisweet chocolate chips (6 oz.)

1 Heat oven to 325°F. Spray 9-inch springform pan with nonstick cooking spray. Press cookie crumbs into bottom of pan.

2 In large bowl, beat cream cheese at medium speed until almost smooth. Add sugar; beat just until mixture is smooth. Beat in vanilla, almond extract and eggs one at a time, beating just until blended.

3 Pour one-third cup of the batter over crumbs; sprinkle with one-half of the cherries. Repeat layers and top with remaining one-third of batter. Bake 1¼ hours or until toothpick inserted in center comes out clean. Remove from oven; cool on wire rack. Cover and refrigerate at least 3 hours.

4 In medium saucepan, heat cream until steaming. Remove from heat; stir in chocolate until melted and smooth. Remove sides of springform pan; place cake on parchment paper. Pour and spread chocolate over top of cake.

5 Refrigerate cake about 30 minutes or until chocolate sets. Before serving, garnish with whipped cream and whole cherries, if desired. Cover and refrigerate up to 1 week, or wrap well and freeze up to 2 weeks.

16 servings

COOKIES 'N CREAM CHEESECAKE

JAYNE HOMSHER
CINCINNATI, OHIO

1 1/4 cups chocolate cookie crumbs

1/2 cup unsalted butter, melted

1/4 cup packed brown sugar

1 teaspoon cinnamon

4 (8-oz.) pkg. cream cheese, softened

1 1/2 cups sugar

2 teaspoons flour

6 eggs

3 egg yolks

1 1/3 cups heavy cream

3 teaspoons vanilla

1 1/2 cups chopped cookies

2 cups sour cream

1 cup semisweet chocolate chips (6 oz.)

1 Heat oven to 425°F. Spray 10-inch springform pan with nonstick cooking spray.

2 In large bowl, blend together cookie crumbs, butter, brown sugar and cinnamon. Press mixture into bottom and up sides of pan. Refrigerate until firm, about 1 hour.

3 To prepare filling, beat cream cheese at low speed in another large bowl until smooth. Beat in 1 1/4 cups of the sugar and flour until well blended. Beat in eggs and egg yolks until mixture is smooth. Stir in cream and 1 teaspoon of the vanilla. Pour one-half of mixture into prepared crust. Sprinkle with chopped cookies. Pour remaining batter over chopped cookies; smooth with spatula. Bake 15 minutes. Reduce oven temperature to 225°F; bake 50 minutes. Increase oven temperature to 350°F.

4 In small bowl, blend together sour cream, remaining 1/4 cup sugar and 1 teaspoon of the vanilla. Spread over cheesecake. Bake 7 minutes. Refrigerate immediately. Cover cheesecake and refrigerate overnight.

5 To prepare frosting, scald 2 cups sour cream in heavy saucepan over medium heat. Add chocolate and remaining 1 teaspoon vanilla; stir until melted. Refrigerate 10 minutes. Set cake on platter; remove springform pan. Refrigerate until ready to serve. Store in refrigerator.

20 servings

DESSERT PIZZA

SHIRLEY MACCLAY
PHILADELPHIA, PENNSYLVANIA

1/2 cup butter

1/2 cup packed brown sugar

1/2 cup sugar

1 egg

1 teaspoon vanilla

1 teaspoon water

1 1/2 cups all-purpose flour

1/2 teaspoon baking soda

1/2 teaspoon salt

1 cup semisweet chocolate chips (6 oz.), melted

1 (8-oz.) container frozen whipped topping, thawed

Fresh fruit

1 Heat oven to 350°F.

2 In medium bowl, beat butter, brown sugar and sugar at high speed until fluffy. Add egg, vanilla and water. Stir in flour, baking soda, salt and chocolate; beat at low speed until smooth. Press mixture into 12-inch pizza pan. Bake 15 to 18 minutes or until golden brown. Cool completely.

3 Spread with whipped topping; top with seasonal fruit (kiwi, fresh berries), sliced and neatly arranged. Cut into wedges. Store in refrigerator.

1 (12-slice) pizza

APPLE AUTUMN CHEESECAKE

CLAUDIA WENDEL
FRESNO, CALIFORNIA

1 cup graham-cracker crumbs

3 tablespoons plus about 1 cup sugar

1 teaspoon cinnamon

1/4 cup butter

3/4 cup finely chopped pecans, if desired

2 (8-oz.) pkg. cream cheese, softened

2 eggs

1/2 teaspoon vanilla

4 cups peeled sliced apples

1/4 cup superfine sugar*

1 Heat oven to 350°F. Spray 9-inch springform pan with nonstick cooking spray.

2 In medium bowl, combine crumbs, 3 tablespoons of the sugar, 1/2 teaspoon of the cinnamon, butter and 1/2 cup of the pecans thoroughly; press mixture into pan. Refrigerate crust until filling is prepared.

3 In large bowl, blend cream cheese with 1/2 cup sugar. Add eggs one at a time, mixing well after each addition; add vanilla. Pour mixture into pan. Toss together apples, remaining 1/2 cup sugar, remaining 1/2 teaspoon cinnamon and remaining 1/4 cup pecans. Arrange apple slices on top of cheesecake batter; sprinkle with superfine sugar.

4 Bake 1 hour and 10 minutes or until nearly set. Cool on wire rack. Drizzle with caramel syrup before serving, if desired. Store in refrigerator.

TIP *Superfine sugar can be found with beverage ingredients in the grocery store, or process regular granulated sugar in blender until very finely ground.

12 servings

MINI CHEESECAKES

SUSAN DROBNY
ARLINGTON HEIGHTS, ILLINOIS

12 vanilla wafers

2 (8-oz.) pkg. cream cheese

1 teaspoon vanilla

1/2 cup sugar

2 eggs

1 Heat oven to 325°F. Line 12 (2 1/2 x 1 1/4-inch) muffin cups with foil liners. Place 1 wafer, flat side down, in each cup. Beat cream cheese, vanilla and sugar at medium speed until well blended. Add eggs; mix well. Pour over wafers, filling three-fourths full.

2 Bake 25 minutes. Cool in pan on wire rack; remove from pan when cool and refrigerate. Top with fruit, preserves, nuts or chocolate, if desired. Store in refrigerator.

12 mini cheesecakes

ITALIAN RICOTTA CHEESECAKE

LORRAINE MAGUR
WASHINGTONVILLE, NEW YORK

1/4 cup corn flake crumbs

2 lbs. whole milk ricotta

1 1/2 cups sugar

4 tablespoons all-purpose flour

2 teaspoons vanilla

1 cup sour cream

1 cup heavy cream, whipped

6 eggs

1 Heat oven to 400°F. Spray 9-inch springform pan with nonstick cooking spray. Sprinkle corn flake crumbs into bottom of pan.

2 In large bowl, mix ricotta, sugar, flour, vanilla, sour cream, whipped cream and eggs thoroughly with wooden spoon, adding eggs one at a time. Pour batter into pan.

3 Bake 1 hour. Turn off oven; let cheesecake cool in oven 20 minutes. Remove from oven; cool on wire rack. Serve with fruit topping, if desired. Store in refrigerator.

12 servings

MINI CHEESECAKES

COMPANY CHEESECAKE

BONNIE E. BARNES
CAMBRIA, CALIFORNIA

CRUST

2 cups crushed vanilla wafers

2 tablespoons sugar

4 tablespoons melted butter

FILLING

2 (8-oz.) plus 1 (3-oz.) pkg. cream cheese

1 cup sugar

2 teaspoons vanilla

2 teaspoons grated lemon peel

3 eggs

TOPPING

2 cups sour cream

1 cup sugar

$1/2$ cup sliced almonds

1 tablespoon cinnamon

1 Heat oven to 350°F.

2 To prepare crust, in medium bowl, combine wafers, 2 tablespoons sugar and butter. Press mixture into bottom of 9-inch springform pan. Bake 10 minutes; set aside.

3 In large bowl, beat cream cheese at medium speed until smooth. Add 1 cup sugar gradually; add vanilla and lemon peel. Beat in eggs one at a time. Pour mixture into crust. Reduce oven temperature to 300°F. Bake 1 hour.

4 To prepare topping, mix together sour cream and 1 cup sugar in another large bowl. Pour over cheesecake. Sprinkle sliced almonds and cinnamon over topping. Bake 10 minutes. Cool; refrigerate until serving. Store in refrigerator.

12 servings

ALMOND-BUTTER TORTE

PATRICIA LENKEN
MILWAUKEE, WISCONSIN

MERINGUE

6 egg whites

$1/4$ teaspoon cream of tartar

2 teaspoons vanilla

$1 1/2$ cups sugar

1 cup toasted slivered almonds, finely chopped

TOPPING

$1 1/2$ cups heavy cream

2 tablespoons powdered sugar

1 teaspoon vanilla

COFFEE-BUTTER CREAM

4 egg yolks

$1/3$ cup milk

2 tablespoons sugar

1 teaspoon instant coffee

$3/4$ cup butter, softened

1 Heat oven to 275°F. Line 2 baking sheets with parchment paper; using 8-inch round cake pan as a guide, draw 4 circles on parchment.

2 Beat egg whites and cream of tartar at medium speed until foamy and double in volume. Sprinkle in 2 teaspoons vanilla and $1 1/2$ cups sugar, 1 tablespoon at a time, beating constantly, until sugar is completely dissolved and firm peaks form. Fold in chopped almonds.

3 Spoon into 4 circles on baking sheets, dividing evenly. Spread into thin, even rounds with spatula. Bake 1 hour or until firm. Turn off oven; cool completely in oven. Remove carefully from parchment paper with spatula or long-blade knife.

4 At least 6 hours before serving, prepare coffee-butter cream. In small bowl over pan of simmering water, beat egg yolks slightly; beat in milk and sugar. Cook, stirring constantly, 10 minutes or until custard thickens and coats metal spoon; remove from heat. Stir in instant coffee; cool completely. Beat butter at medium speed until very soft and creamy. Beat in cooled custard, 1 tablespoon at a time, beating well after each addition until mixture is creamy-thick.

5 To prepare topping, beat cream in medium bowl with powdered sugar and 1 teaspoon vanilla until stiff. Place one meringue layer on large serving plate; spread with one-third of coffee-butter cream mixture and one-fourth of topping mixture. Repeat with remaining layers and filling, stacking on top of first layer. Swirl remaining whipped cream on top. Garnish with more toasted slivered almonds. Refrigerate until serving. Store in refrigerator.

8 to 10 servings

CHOCOLATE CHEESECAKE

BOBBI BARBARESE
MOORESTOWN, NEW JERSEY

1 1/3 cups chocolate cookie crumbs

3 tablespoons melted butter

2 (8-oz.) pkg. cream cheese, softened

1 1/4 cups plus 2 tablespoons sugar

1/3 cup unsweetened cocoa

1 1/2 teaspoons vanilla

2 eggs

1 cup sour cream

1 Heat oven to 350°F.

2 In medium bowl, blend together crumbs and butter mixture; press mixture into bottom and partially up sides of 9-inch springform pan; refrigerate.

3 In large bowl, beat cream cheese at high speed until smooth. Beat in 1 1/4 cups of the sugar and cocoa at medium speed. Add 1 teaspoon of the vanilla and eggs; continue beating at medium speed until smooth. Pour mixture into pan. Bake 35 minutes.

4 To prepare frosting, combine sour cream, remaining 2 tablespoons sugar and remaining 1/2 teaspoon vanilla in large bowl. Spread over top of hot cheesecake. Return to oven; bake an additional 10 minutes. Shave bittersweet chocolate over cake while still warm, if desired. Cool completely in pan on wire rack. Refrigerate until ready to serve. Store in refrigerator.

12 servings

PEANUT BUTTER CHEESECAKE

CAROL HAWLEY
FREDERICK, MARYLAND

CRUST

1 1/2 cups crushed pretzels

1/3 cup melted butter

FILLING

5 (8-oz.) pkg. cream cheese, softened

1 1/2 cups sugar

3/4 cup creamy peanut butter

2 teaspoons vanilla

3 eggs

1 cup peanut butter chips (6 oz.)

1 cup semisweet chocolate chips (6 oz.)

TOPPING

1 cup sour cream

1/2 cup sugar

2 tablespoons creamy peanut butter

1/2 cup finely chopped unsalted peanuts

1 Heat oven to 350°F. Spray 10-inch springform pan with nonstick cooking spray.

2 In small bowl, blend together pretzels and butter. Press into bottom and 1 inch up sides of pan. Bake 5 minutes; cool on wire rack.

3 In large bowl, beat cream cheese and 1 1/2 cups sugar at high speed until smooth. Add 3/4 cup peanut butter and vanilla; mix well. Add eggs; beat at low speed just until combined. Stir in chips. Pour mixture into crust; bake 50 to 55 minutes or until almost set. Cool on wire rack 15 minutes.

4 To prepare topping, combine sour cream, 1/2 cup sugar and 2 tablespoons peanut butter in large bowl; spread over warm cheesecake. Sprinkle with peanuts. Return to oven; bake an additional 5 minutes. Cool on wire rack 10 minutes. Carefully run thin knife around edge of pan to loosen; cool 1 hour. Refrigerate overnight. Store in refrigerator.

16 servings

WINE-BRAISED PEAR CHANTILLY

WINE-BRAISED PEAR CHANTILLY

MRS. ROBERT WOOD
HOLLY HILL, FLORIDA

4 ripe pears (Anjou, Bartlett or Bosc)

3 cups dry red wine (cabernet, merlot or zinfandel)

2 tablespoons sugar

2 sticks cinnamon

4 whole cloves

$\frac{1}{4}$ teaspoon ground nutmeg

4 ($\frac{1}{2}$-inch) slices pound cake

1 cup heavy cream

2 tablespoons powdered sugar

1 teaspoon vanilla

$\frac{1}{4}$ cup sliced butter-toasted almonds

1 Peel and core pears, leaving stems intact. Place pears in non-reactive Dutch oven with wine, sugar, cinnamon, cloves and nutmeg. Simmer 20 minutes. Remove pears; cool in refrigerator.

2 Simmer wine mixture until reduced to 2 cups syrup. Place cake slices in 4 dessert bowls, splashed with $\frac{1}{4}$ cup orange liqueur, if desired.

3 In medium bowl, beat cream at medium speed until soft peaks form. Beat in powdered sugar and vanilla.

4 Place pears upright on cake slices; trim bottoms to stand, if necessary. Remove cinnamon sticks and cloves; pour syrup over pears. Garnish with whipped cream; coat with almond slices. Serve with sweet wine or champagne. Store in refrigerator.

4 servings

CHOCOLATE CARAMEL CHEESECAKE

JENNY DIBLEY
MIDDLEBURY, INDIANA

CRUST

$\frac{1}{2}$ cup semisweet chocolate chips (3 oz.)

$\frac{1}{3}$ cup butter

1 $\frac{1}{2}$ cups old-fashioned or quick-cooking oats

$\frac{1}{2}$ cup plus 1 tablespoon all-purpose flour

$\frac{1}{4}$ cup packed brown sugar

FILLING

2 (8-oz.) pkg. cream cheese, softened

$\frac{2}{3}$ cup sugar

1 teaspoon vanilla

2 eggs

$\frac{1}{2}$ cup semisweet chocolate chips (3 oz.)

1 cup caramel topping

1 tablespoon all-purpose flour

$\frac{1}{2}$ cup fudge topping

$\frac{1}{2}$ cup crushed pecans

1 Heat oven to 350°F. Spray bottom and sides of 9-inch springform pan with nonstick cooking spray.

2 To prepare crust, melt $\frac{1}{2}$ cup chocolate chips and butter in large saucepan over low heat; cool slightly. Stir in oats, $\frac{1}{2}$ cup flour and brown sugar; mix well. Press firmly into bottom and 1 inch up sides of pan. Bake 10 minutes; cool completely.

3 To prepare filling, beat cream cheese, sugar and vanilla in large bowl at medium speed until creamy. Add eggs one at a time, beating well after each addition. Stir in remaining $\frac{1}{2}$ cup chocolate chips. Pour mixture over crust. Combine $\frac{1}{3}$ cup of the caramel topping and remaining 1 tablespoon flour; mix well. Spoon mixture over filling; swirl with knife. Bake 40 to 50 minutes or until center is set; cool on wire rack. Refrigerate 6 hours or overnight.

4 To serve, drizzle with remaining $\frac{2}{3}$ cup caramel and fudge toppings. Sprinkle pecans over top. Store covered in refrigerator.

12 servings

ALMOND-FLAVORED LIQUEUR CHEESECAKE

RITA HASHEMI
DUBLIN, OHIO

1 1/2 cups graham-cracker crumbs

1 1/4 cups plus 1/3 cup sugar

1/2 cup melted butter

4 (8-oz.) pkg. cream cheese, softened

sugar

4 eggs

1 cup sour cream

1/2 cup almond-flavored liqueur

1 Heat oven to 325°F.

2 In large bowl, combine crumbs, 1/3 cup sugar and butter. Press mixture into bottom of 9-inch spring-form pan; refrigerate.

3 In food processor, blend cream cheese, remaining 1 1/4 cups sugar, eggs and sour cream until completely smooth. Blend in liqueur. Pour over refrigerated crust.

4 Place 8-inch square pan filled halfway with hot water on lower rack of oven. Bake cheesecake on middle rack of oven 1 1/4 hours until almost set. Turn oven off. Cool cheesecake in oven 1 hour. Remove from oven; cool to room temperature on wire rack. Store in refrigerator.

16 servings

CHOCOLATE LOVERS' CHOCOLATE CHIP DREAM CHEESECAKE

JENNIFER VERRA
JERSEY CITY, NEW JERSEY

CAKE

1 (8-oz.) pkg. cream cheese, softened

1 (14-oz.) can sweetened condensed milk

1 egg

1 tablespoon vanilla

1 cup semisweet chocolate chips (6 oz.)

1 teaspoon all-purpose flour

1 (9-inch) chocolate pie shell

CHOCOLATE GLAZE

1/2 cup semisweet chocolate chips (3 oz.)

1/4 cup plus 2 tablespoons heavy cream

1/4 cup white chocolate chips (1 1/2 oz.)

1 Heat oven to 350°F.

2 In large bowl, beat cream cheese at medium speed until fluffy. Slowly add milk; beat until smooth. Add egg and vanilla; mix well. Toss 1 cup chocolate chips with flour. Add to cheesecake mixture; stir well. Pour mixture into pie shell.

3 Bake about 35 minutes or until center springs back when lightly touched. Cool.

4 To prepare glaze, combine 1/2 chocolate chips with 1/4 cup of the cream in large saucepan; melt over low heat until smooth and glossy. Pour over cheesecake. Refrigerate 1 hour or until glaze is set.

5 In medium saucepan, melt white chocolate chips with remaining 2 tablespoons cream; drop in 3 places over chocolate glaze. Swirl lightly with fork or knife. Store in refrigerator.

12 servings

PEPPERMINT CANDY CHEESECAKE

KATHERINE PRICE
SHOW LOW, ARIZONA

1 cup graham-cracker crumbs

3/4 cup sugar

1/4 cup plus 2 tablespoons melted butter

1 1/2 cups sour cream

2 eggs

1 tablespoon all-purpose flour

2 teaspoons vanilla

2 (8-oz.) pkg. cream cheese, softened

1/2 cup crushed peppermint candy

1 Heat oven to 325°F.

2 In large bowl, combine crumbs, 1/4 cup of the sugar and 1/4 cup of the butter; mix well. Press mixture into bottom of 9-inch springform pan.

3 In blender, combine sour cream, remaining 1/2 cup sugar, eggs, flour and vanilla; process until smooth. Add cream cheese; process until smooth. Blend in remaining 2 tablespoons butter and crushed candy. Pour into crust.

4 Bake 45 minutes. Refrigerate at least 4 hours before serving. Store in refrigerator.

12 servings

DUTCH OLIEBOLLEN

THERESA GAEDTKE
LUXEMBURG, WISCONSIN

3 1/4 cups all-purpose flour

2 (1/4-oz.) pkg. active dry yeast

1 cup milk

1/4 cup shortening

1/3 cup sugar

1 teaspoon salt

1 teaspoon vanilla

2 eggs

3 egg yolks

1/2 cup raisins

1/2 cup chopped mixed candied fruit

Vegetable oil

1/2 cup powdered sugar, if desired

1 teaspoon cinnamon, if desired

1 In large bowl, combine 2 cups of the flour and yeast. In small saucepan, heat milk, shortening, sugar and salt just until warm. Stir occasionally until shortening almost melts. Stir in vanilla. Add milk mixture, eggs and egg yolks to dry ingredients in bowl. Beat at low speed 1 to 2 minutes, scraping sides of bowl frequently. Beat 3 minutes at high speed. Stir in remaining 1 1/4 cups flour, raisins and fruit.

2 Cover and let rise about 30 minutes or until doubled in size. In large pot, heat 4 inches vegetable oil to 350°F. Drop dough by tablespoonfuls into hot oil; cook until browned. Drain on paper towel or brown paper bag; dust with powdered sugar or sugar-cinnamon mixture. Store in refrigerator.

About 2 dozen

SOPAIPILLAS

CHERYL BARNA
WOODBRIDGE, VIRGINIA

1 (¼-oz.) pkg. active dry yeast

3 teaspoons sugar

1½ cups warm water (105°F to 115°F)

1 tablespoon shortening, melted

1 teaspoon baking powder

1 teaspoon salt

4 cups all-purpose flour

Vegetable oil

1 In large bowl, dissolve yeast and 1 teaspoon of the sugar in water; let stand 5 minutes or until bubbly. Add remaining 2 teaspoons sugar, shortening, baking powder, salt and 2 cups of the flour; beat at high speed until smooth. Stir in remaining 2 cups flour to make soft dough.

2 Place dough in greased bowl, turning to grease top. Cover and let rise in warm place 1 hour or until doubled.

3 Fill large pot with 4 inches vegetable oil. Heat to 375°F. Meanwhile, punch dough down. Turn out onto lightly floured surface; let rest 5 minutes. Knead 4 to 5 times. Roll dough to ¼ inch thickness; cut into 3-inch squares. Cut each square diagonally to form 2 triangles.

4 Gently drop 2 to 3 dough triangles at a time into oil; turning once. Cook until sopaipillas are golden brown. Drain on paper towels. Serve hot with honey or powdered sugar, if desired. Store in refrigerator.

3 dozen

CLAUDIA'S PUMPKIN-TOFFEE CHEESECAKE

CLAUDIA WENDEL
FRESNO, CALIFORNIA

CRUST

¼ cup melted butter

1¾ cups finely crushed pecan-shortbread

⅓ cup toffee bits

CHEESECAKE

3 (8-oz.) pkg. cream cheese, softened

¾ cup packed brown sugar

1 cup sugar

¾ cup solid pack pumpkin puree, blended smooth before measuring

2 large eggs

2 tablespoons corn-starch

½ teaspoon pumpkin pie spice

⅓ cup heavy cream

⅔ cup toffee bits

TOPPING

2 cups sour cream

¼ cup sugar

½ teaspoon vanilla

⅓ cup caramel syrup

⅓ cup toffee bits

1 Heat oven to 350°F.

2 To prepare crust, in medium bowl, combine butter and cookie crumbs; stir well and press into bottom and slightly up edges of 9-inch springform pan. Sprinkle ⅓ cup toffee bits over crust. Bake 6 to 8 minutes; do not brown. Set aside to cool or refrigerate until ready to use.

3 To prepare cheesecake, in large bowl, combine cream cheese with brown sugar and 1 cup sugar until creamy. Add pumpkin and eggs; beat until smooth. Beat in cornstarch and pie spice. Stir in cream and ⅔ cup toffee bits. Pour pumpkin mixture carefully into crust. Bake about 1¼ hours or until nearly set; center will slightly jiggle when shaken.

4 To prepare topping, mix sour cream, ¼ cup sugar and vanilla in medium bowl. Remove cake from oven; spread topping on warm cheesecake. Return to oven; bake an additional 8 minutes. Do not brown. Turn oven off; leave cheesecake in oven 1 hour. Refrigerate several hours or overnight. Remove from pan; place on cake platter.

5 Just before serving, drizzle ⅓ cup caramel syrup over cheesecake; top with ⅓ cup toffee bits. Garnish with whipped cream, if desired. Store in refrigerator.

16 servings

CLAUDIA'S PUMPKIN-TOFFEE CHEESECAKE

BLACK & WHITE CHEESECAKE

JOYCE QUICK
CANDOR, NEW YORK

PASTRY

6 tablespoons unsalted butter, softened

1/2 cup sugar

3/4 teaspoon vanilla

1/8 teaspoon salt

1/4 cup plus 2 tablespoons unsweetened cocoa

3/4 cup all-purpose flour

FILLING

1 cup semisweet chocolate chips (6 oz.)

1/4 cup water

3 (8-oz.) pkg. cream cheese, softened

1 1/4 cups sugar

1/2 teaspoon vanilla

2 eggs

1 Heat oven to 350°F.

2 To prepare pastry, in food processor, combine butter, 1/2 cup sugar, 3/4 teaspoon vanilla and salt; process until smooth. Blend in cocoa just until dark smooth paste forms. Mix in flour until just incorporated but still crumbly.

3 Firmly press three-fourths of the pastry into bottom of 9-inch springform pan. Crumble remaining pastry into shallow baking pan.

4 Bake both pans 10 minutes. Remove pan of extra crumbs; bake crust an additional 5 minutes. Cool pans on wire rack. Place cooled crumbs from baking pan in food processor; pulse until pulverized. Store in container; set aside.

5 To prepare filling, melt chocolate chips with water over low heat in small saucepan, stirring occasionally until smooth. Cover saucepan to keep warm; set aside. In large bowl, beat cream cheese at medium speed until smooth. Add 1 1/4 cups sugar gradually, beating just until smooth. Add vanilla and eggs, one at a time, beating just until mixed. Set aside 1 cup batter.

6 Pour remaining batter into crust. Stir warm chocolate into reserved batter. Pour thick ring about 1/2 inch from side of pan, on top of plain batter, leaving a "bullseye" of plain batter in center. Pull knife through both batters to marble.

7 Bake 1 hour and 10 minutes or until toothpick inserted in center comes out clean. Run a thin knife carefully around edges to release cake from side of pan. Cool in pan on wire rack; place inverted large bowl over cheesecake on wire rack while cooling. To serve, remove sides of pan. Press reserved pastry crumbs around side of cake, being careful not to get crumbs on top. Store in refrigerator.

12 servings

COOKIES AND CREAM CHEESECAKE WITH WHITE CHOCOLATE

CLAUDIA WENDEL
FRESNO, CALIFORNIA

2 cups finely crushed chocolate or vanilla wafer cookies

3/4 cup plus 3 tablespoons sugar

1/4 cup melted butter

1 (4-oz.) white chocolate baking bar

2 (8-oz.) pkg. cream cheese, softened

1 1/2 cups sour cream

2 eggs

10 cream-filled chocolate sandwich cookies, broken into thirds

1/4 cup all-purpose flour

1 Heat oven to 325°F. Spray 9-inch springform pan with nonstick cooking spray.

2 In medium bowl, mix cookie crumbs and 3 tablespoons of the sugar. Add butter; mix until well blended. Press mixture into pan. Set aside.

3 In small saucepan, melt white chocolate over low heat, stirring frequently, until smooth. Cool slightly. Beat cream cheese until fluffy. Beat in sour cream and remaining 3/4 cup sugar. Add eggs one at a time, beating well after each addition. Stir in melted white chocolate. Toss cookies in flour; fold into cheese mixture carefully.

4 Bake 50 to 60 minutes or until set. Turn oven off. Leave cheesecake in oven 1 hour with oven door partially open. Cool an additional 1 hour on wire rack. Decorate with cream cheese frosting around edges, hiding any cracks with whole or coarsely broken sandwich cookies. Store in refrigerator.

12 servings

APPLE RING DESSERT FRITTERS

GWEN CAMPBELL
STERLING, VIRGINIA

FRITTERS

4 to 6 Granny Smith apples

1 cup all-purpose flour

1 teaspoon baking powder

1 tablespoon sugar

1/4 teaspoon salt

1/4 teaspoon ground cinnamon

1 egg

1/2 cup milk

1 tablespoon vegetable oil

1 tablespoon fresh lemon juice

1 cup flaked coconut

Vegetable oil

TOPPING

1 tablespoon cornstarch

1/4 cup sugar

1/8 teaspoon salt

1 cup water

2 tablespoons vanilla

2 tablespoons butter

1/4 teaspoon nutmeg

1 Peel and core apples; slice into crosswise 1/4-inch rings.

2 In large bowl, mix together flour, baking powder, 1 tablespoon of the sugar, 1/4 teaspoon salt and cinnamon. In a small bowl, lightly beat egg, milk and oil; stir into flour mixture. Stir in lemon juice and coconut.

3 In large pot, heat 3 inches oil to 350°F. Dip each apple ring in batter. Fry in hot oil until golden brown on both sides. Drain on paper towels.

4 To prepare topping, combine cornstarch, 1/4 cup sugar, 1/8 teaspoon salt, water, vanilla, butter and nutmeg in small saucepan. Cook over low heat, stirring frequently, until thickened. Drizzle over fritters. Store in refrigerator.

About 2 dozen

& SAUCES

GINGER-PEACHY ICE CREAM *(page 148)*

PISTACHIO TORTE

FRANCES FRANCO
MELBOURNE BEACH, FLORIDA

1 cup all-purpose flour

$^1/2$ cup butter, softened

2 tablespoons sugar

1 cup chopped nuts

1 (8-oz.) pkg. cream cheese, softened

$^2/3$ cup powdered sugar

1 (8-oz.) container frozen whipped topping, thawed

2 (3.4-oz.) pkg. instant pistachio pudding mix

$2^1/4$ cups cold milk

1 Heat oven to 375°F.

2 In large bowl, mix flour, butter, sugar and $^1/2$ cup of the chopped nuts until crumbly. Press into 13x9-inch pan. Bake 10 to 15 minutes or until lightly browned.

3 In another large bowl, beat cream cheese, powdered sugar and one-half of the whipped topping at medium speed 2 minutes. Spread over cooled crust.

4 In another bowl, combine pudding mix and milk. Beat 2 minutes on medium-low speed until thickened; spread on cream cheese layer.

5 To prepare topping, spread remaining whipped topping over pudding layer. Sprinkle with remaining $^1/2$ cup chopped nuts. Store in refrigerator.

16 servings

LAYERED CHOCOLATE MOUSSE DESSERT

MARIE ROBERTSON
HODGEVILLE, KENTUCKY

FIRST LAYER

1 cup all-purpose flour

$^1/2$ cup softened butter

2 tablespoons sugar

SECOND LAYER

1 (8-oz.) pkg. cream cheese

1 cup powdered sugar

1 (16-oz.) container frozen whipped topping, thawed

THIRD LAYER

1 (3.4-oz.) pkg. instant chocolate pudding mix

1 (3.4-oz.) pkg. instant vanilla pudding mix

3 cups milk

1 Heat oven to 350°F. In medium bowl, combine flour, butter and sugar; mix well. Press mixture into 10-inch springform pan. Bake 15 minutes or until golden brown. Cool. This is the first layer (crust).

2 In large bowl, beat cream cheese and powdered sugar at medium speed until fluffy. Fold in 1 cup of the whipped topping. Spread mixture over cooled crust. This is the second layer.

3 In another large bowl, combine chocolate and vanilla pudding mixes with milk; whisk together until thickened. Spread over cream cheese layer. This is the third layer.

4 Spread remaining 1 cup whipped topping over pudding mixture. Garnish with grated chocolate, if desired. Store in refrigerator.

TIP *Lemon pudding can be substituted for chocolate and vanilla puddings.

16 servings

BLACK BOMBE CAKE

JOAN DEADY
SAN FRANCISCO, CALIFORNIA

½ cup freshly brewed coffee

1 cup semisweet chocolate chips (6 oz.)

4 eggs

1 cup plus 2 tablespoons packed brown sugar

1 cup butter, softened

4 tablespoons dark rum

1 cup heavy cream, whipped

½ cup sliced fresh strawberries

1 Heat oven to 350°F. Using ovenproof mixing bowl with narrow bottom, form aluminum foil mold by turning 6- to 8-cup bowl upside down. Tear off 12-inch square of foil; center over inverted bowl. With hands, press down on all sides around bowl to form foil into bowl shape. Remove foil; turn bowl right-side-up. Place foil bowl inside bowl; press into place.

2 In small saucepan, combine coffee and chocolate chips over low heat until chocolate is melted. In large bowl, beat eggs at medium speed. Beat in 1 cup of the brown sugar, butter, 2 tablespoons of the rum and chocolate mixture; blend until smooth. Pour mixture into foil-lined bowl. Bake 55 to 60 minutes or until top crust is cracked.

3 Remove from oven; cool 2 minutes on wire rack. Place parchment paper over top; place fingers on paper; press raised edges of cake down to make flat surface. Cover airtight; refrigerate overnight.

4 To serve, remove covering; place plate over top of bowl, invert bowl and plate. Remove bowl; remove foil. Stir remaining 2 tablespoons brown sugar and remaining 2 tablespoons rum to whipped cream. Spread whipped cream over cake. Distribute strawberries evenly over topping. Cut into thin slices to serve. Store in refrigerator.

10 servings

PEGGY'S MINT ICE CREAM DESSERT

PEGGY WINKWORTH
DURANGO, COLORADO

1 ¼ cups crushed chocolate sandwich cookies

¼ cup melted butter

1 (4-oz.) bar German sweet chocolate

½ cup butter

⅔ cup sugar

⅛ teaspoon salt

⅔ cup evaporated milk

1 teaspoon vanilla

1 quart mint chocolate chip or vanilla ice cream

1 In large bowl, combine crushed cookies and melted butter; mix well. Reserve ⅔ cup. Press remaining crumb mixture into 9-inch springform pan; refrigerate.

2 In small saucepan, combine chocolate, butter, sugar, salt and milk. Bring to a boil; cook 4 minutes. Remove from heat. Stir in vanilla; cool. Spread mixture over crust. Chill in freezer until set.

3 When torte layer is set, serve with ice cream and reserved cookie crumbs. Store in freezer. Thaw slightly to cut and serve.

12 servings

PEANUT CREAM DREAM

DAWN SLATEM
SALEM, OREGON

8 to 9 whole chocolate-covered graham crackers or chocolate graham crackers

1½ cups honey-roasted peanuts

1 quart Neapolitan ice cream, softened

1 Line 9-inch springform pan with chocolate-covered graham crackers, breaking crackers as needed to completely cover bottom. Sprinkle honey-roasted peanuts over crackers. Spread Neapolitan ice cream on top. Freeze 2 hours.

2 Top each serving with whipped cream and one spoonful strawberry jam, if desired. Store in refrigerator.

16 servings

LEMON SHERBET ICE CREAM

NANCY WIKE
HUDSONVILLE, MICHIGAN

1¼ cups fresh lemon juice

¾ cup fresh orange juice

4½ cups sugar

2 quarts milk

1 (12-oz.) can evaporated milk

In large bowl, combine lemon juice, orange juice, sugar, milk and evaporated milk; mix until well blended. Freeze according to your ice cream maker's directions. (Do this in two batches.)

About 3 quarts

FROZEN PUDDING SANDWICHES

JUDY MANGES
HORNELL, NEW YORK

1½ cups cold milk

½ cup peanut butter

1 (3.4-oz.) pkg. instant vanilla or chocolate pudding mix

24 whole regular or cinnamon graham crackers or 48 chocolate wafer cookies

1 In large bowl, add milk gradually to peanut butter, beating at medium speed until smooth. Add pudding mix; beat slowly on low speed about 2 minutes or until thickened. Let stand 5 minutes.

2 Generously spread filling over one-half of the crackers or cookies. Top with remaining crackers or cookies, pressing lightly and smoothing around edges with spatula. Freeze about 3 hours or until firm. Wrap individual sandwiches in plastic wrap; store in freezer.

12 servings

PEANUT BUTTER ICE CREAM TOPPING

TAMMY RAYNES
NATCHITOCHES, LOUISIANA

1 cup packed brown sugar

½ cup light corn syrup

3 tablespoons butter

⅛ teaspoon salt

1 cup creamy peanut butter

½ cup evaporated milk

1 Combine brown sugar, syrup, butter and salt in medium microwave-safe dish. Cover and microwave on High 4 minutes or until mixture boils, stirring twice. Add peanut butter; stir until smooth. Stir in milk.

2 Serve warm over ice cream; sprinkle with peanuts, if desired. Cover and store sauce in refrigerator. To reheat, microwave on Medium power 1 to 2 minutes or until thoroughly heated.

About 2½ cups

FROZEN PUDDING SANDWICHES

CHERRY POUND PARFAITS

CHERRY POUND PARFAITS

CHRISTINA THOMPSON
PORTSMOUTH, VIRGINIA

1 (10¾-oz.) frozen pound cake, cut into 1-inch cubes

1 pint cherry or vanilla ice cream

1 (16-oz.) bag frozen dark sweet cherries, thawed

¼ cup chocolate syrup

2 tablespoons chopped walnuts or pecans

Divide one-half of the cake cubes among four parfait glasses. Top with one-half of the ice cream and one-half of the cherries. Repeat layers with remaining cake, ice cream and cherries. Drizzle syrup over each dessert; sprinkle with nuts.

4 servings

PEANUT BUSTER PARFAIT

JUNE POEPPING
QUINCY, ILLINOIS

1 (1-lb. 5-oz.) pkg. brownie mix

½ gallon vanilla ice cream, softened

1 (16-oz.) jar hot fudge sauce

2 cups dry-roasted peanuts

1 Bake brownies in 13x9-inch pan according to package directions. Cool completely on wire rack.

2 Spread vanilla ice cream over cooled brownies. Spoon fudge sauce over ice cream. Sprinkle with peanuts. Freeze 2 hours or until firm. Remove from freezer 15 minutes before serving. Cut into squares.

16 servings

FROZEN MOCHA CHEESECAKE

PAMELA DAVIS
EGG HARBOR, WISCONSIN

1¼ cups chocolate wafer crumbs

¼ cup sugar

¼ cup melted butter

1 (8-oz.) pkg. cream cheese

1 (14-oz.) can sweetened condensed milk

⅔ cup chocolate syrup

1 tablespoon instant coffee, dissolved in ½ teaspoon hot water

2 cups heavy cream, whipped

Chocolate-covered coffee beans

1 Spray 9-inch springform pan with nonstick cooking spray.

2 In large bowl, mix crumbs, sugar and butter. Press mixture firmly into bottom and 1 inch up sides of pan.

3 In another large bowl, beat cream cheese at medium speed until fluffy; add sweetened condensed milk and chocolate syrup. Stir in coffee. Fold in whipped cream. Pour into pan. Freeze at least 6 hours. Garnish with chocolate-covered coffee beans, if desired. Store in freezer.

12 servings

FROZEN CITRUS PIE

CHERYL PETERSON

½ (12-oz.) can frozen concentrated orange juice, lemonade or pink lemonade

1 pint vanilla ice cream, softened

1 (8-oz.) container frozen whipped topping, thawed

1 (6-oz.) graham-cracker pie crust

In large bowl, beat frozen concentrate at high speed about 30 seconds. Blend in ice cream. Fold in whipped topping until smooth. Pour into prepared crust. Freeze until firm.

8 servings

ICE CREAM PIE

JUDY SCHOENING
GREENFIELD, WISCONSIN

3 cups crisp rice cereal

1/3 cup maple syrup

1/3 cup chunky peanut butter

1 quart ice cream, softened

Ice cream toppings

In large bowl, combine cereal, syrup and peanut butter. Spread in bottom and up sides of 9-inch pie pan. Spread ice cream of choice over crust; add toppings of choice. Cover with aluminum foil; freeze.

12 servings

COOL AND TANGY LIME CREAM SHERBET

GWEN CAMPBELL
STERLING, VIRGINIA

1 (1/4 oz.) pkg. sugar-free lime-flavored gelatin

2 cups milk

1/2 teaspoon salt

1 1/3 cups sugar

2 cups half-and-half

6 1/4 teaspoons grated lime peel

1/2 cup fresh lime juice

1/3 cup fresh lemon juice

Green food coloring

1 Sprinkle gelatin over 1/2 cup of the milk in heatproof cup; let stand until softened. Place gelatin mixture over boiling water until gelatin dissolves.

2 In large bowl, combine remaining 1 1/2 cups milk, salt, sugar, half-and-half, lime peel, lime juice, lemon juice and a few drops of food coloring. Stir together thoroughly. Pour mixture into 15x10x1-inch baking pan; place pan in freezer.

3 When frozen 1 inch from edge, transfer mixture to large chilled bowl; beat at medium speed until smooth. Spread mixture into pan; cover with aluminum foil. Refreeze. Garnish with lime slices.

16 servings

GINGER-PEACHY ICE CREAM

MRS. ROBERT WOOD
HOLLY HILL, FLORIDA

4 ripe peaches*

2 cups half-and-half

2 cups heavy cream

1 teaspoon vanilla

1/2 cup sugar

1/4 cup chopped crystallized ginger

1/8 teaspoon salt

1 Peel, pit and mash peaches. Open pits with nutcrackers or hammer. Discard shells and finely mince kernels, adding them to mashed peaches.

2 In churn, combine half-and-half, cream and vanilla; freeze to slush consistency. Add peach mixture, sugar, ginger and salt. Follow manufacturer's directions to continue freezing ice cream.

TIP *1/4 teaspoon almond extract can be substituted for peach kernels.

About 1 1/2 quarts

PRALINE ICE CREAM SAUCE

TAMMY RAYNES
NATCHITOCHES, LOUISIANA

1/4 cup butter

1 1/4 cups packed brown sugar

3/4 cup light corn syrup

3 tablespoons all-purpose flour

1 1/2 cups chopped pecans

2/3 cup evaporated milk

In medium saucepan, melt butter over medium heat. Stir in brown sugar, syrup and flour. Bring mixture to a boil; reduce heat and simmer, stirring constantly with wire whisk, about 5 minutes. Remove from heat; cool 10 minutes. Stir in pecans and evaporated milk. Serve sauce immediately over ice cream.

About 2 1/2 cups

GINGER-PEACHY ICE CREAM

CRANBERRY ICE

PATTY RODERICK
JEFFERSON CITY, MISSOURI

2 cups fresh cranberries

2$\frac{1}{2}$ cups water

1$\frac{1}{3}$ cups sugar

$\frac{1}{8}$ teaspoon salt

1 Place cranberries in medium saucepan; add water. Cook over medium-low heat 8 to 10 minutes or until tender and berries begin to burst. Add sugar and salt; cook and stir until sugar is dissolved. Place in food processor or blender; blend until smooth.

2 Pour mixture into 9-inch springform pan. Freeze at least 2 hours or until set. Remove from freezer about 20 minutes before serving. Spoon cranberry ice into sherbet dishes.

4 to 6 servings

MOM'S ICE CREAM CAKE ROLL

LISA THOMPSON
WESTFIELD, MASSACHUSETTS

$\frac{3}{4}$ cup all-purpose flour

1 teaspoon baking powder

1 teaspoon salt

4 eggs, separated

12 tablespoons sugar

1 teaspoon vanilla

2 tablespoons water

$\frac{1}{2}$ gallon ice cream, softened

1 Heat oven to 375°F. Line 15$\frac{1}{2}$x10$\frac{1}{2}$x1-inch baking pan with parchment paper.

2 In large bowl, combine flour, baking powder and salt; set aside. Add egg whites; beat until stiff peaks form. Beat in 6 tablespoons of the sugar, 2 tablespoons at a time; set aside. Beat egg yolks until thick and lemon-colored. Add remaining 6 tablespoons sugar and vanilla. Slowly add water. Stir in flour mixture. Gently fold in egg whites until blended. Spread in pan.

3 Bake 12 minutes, watching carefully that cake does not burn. Remove from oven; invert cake onto clean kitchen towel sprinkled with sugar. Carefully remove parchment paper and roll with towel firmly from short end. Cool completely. Unroll carefully. Spread with softened ice cream and reroll; freeze until firm. Slice roll in 1-inch slices to serve.

16 servings

PEPPERMINT ICE CREAM DESSERT

JENNY DIBLEY
MIDDLEBURY, INDIANA

1 cup all-purpose flour

¼ cup packed brown sugar

½ cup chopped pecans

½ cup butter, melted

1 cup semisweet chocolate chips (6 oz.)

1 cup miniature marshmallows

1 cup evaporated milk

1 (½-gallon) box peppermint bon-bon ice cream

1 Heat oven to 350°F.

2 In large bowl, combine flour, brown sugar, pecans and butter; mix well. Spread and press mixture in 9-inch springform pan. Bake 20 minutes, stirring after first 10 minutes. Let cool, stirring to keep crumbly. Reserve ⅓ cup for topping.

3 In medium saucepan, melt chocolate chips, marshmallows and milk over medium-low heat. Let cool. Open ice cream box fully; slice ice cream into 1-inch-thick slices.

4 Layer slices of ice cream over crust. Spread ice cream until smooth. Drizzle chocolate sauce over ice cream. Add another layer of ice cream with another layer of chocolate sauce; sprinkle with reserved crumb mixture. Freeze about 30 minutes or until set.

12 servings

CHOCOLATE GRAVY

MRS. GLEN CAIN
FORT SMITH, ARKANSAS

¼ cup butter, melted

3 tablespoons all-purpose flour

2 cups milk

⅔ cup sugar

1 teaspoon vanilla

3 tablespoons unsweetened cocoa

In medium saucepan, combine butter, flour, milk, sugar, vanilla and cocoa; mix well. Bring to a boil over low heat until mixture is of desired consistency. Serve over vanilla ice cream, if desired.

About 4 cups

CANDY &

SWEET TREATS

TEXAS PRALINES

TINA YOUNG
ATOKA, OKLAHOMA

3 cups packed brown sugar

1 cup half-and-half

3 tablespoons light corn syrup

1/3 cup butter

1 teaspoon vanilla

1 cup broken pecans

1 Line 2 baking sheets with parchment paper. In large saucepan, combine brown sugar, half-and-half, corn syrup and butter. Heat to a boil over medium-high heat, stirring constantly. Reduce heat to medium-low, stirring occasionally to prevent scorching. Cook until mixture reaches soft ball stage Remove from heat and cool to lukewarm without stirring.

2 Add vanilla; beat until mixture changes color and begins to thicken. Quickly pour mixture onto baking sheets, making 6 circles about 3 1/2 inches in diameter on each baking sheet; cool. (If mixture sets too fast, add 1 teaspoon or more hot water to mixture until patties again spread when poured.) Sprinkle each patty with 1 teaspoon nuts.

1 dozen pralines

MOM'S BUTTERSCOTCH CANDY

KATHY MULLICAN
KEIZER, OREGON

1 1/2 cups sugar

2 teaspoons vinegar

2/3 cup butter

2/3 cup water

1 1/2 teaspoons vanilla

Spray 13x9-inch pan with nonstick cooking spray. In medium saucepan, heat sugar, vinegar, butter and water until boiling. Stir in vanilla and turn quickly into pan. Score into squares; break when cool.

About 3/4 pound

BRIGADIERS

STEPHANIE FISHER-MATHEWS
SARASOTA, FLORIDA

1 (14-oz.) can sweetened condensed milk

5 tablespoons unsweetened cocoa

2/3 cup whole milk

1 tablespoon unsalted butter

Chocolate sprinkles

Unsweetened cocoa

Powdered sugar

1 Spray 13x9-inch pan with nonstick cooking spray. In large saucepan, heat condensed milk, cocoa, whole milk and butter over medium-high heat 20 to 30 minutes, stirring occasionally, until mixture falls away from sides of pan.

2 Pour mixture into pan; spread butter over mixture to prevent crusting. Cool completely.

3 Roll mixture into bite-size balls. Roll balls in chocolate sprinkles or cocoa and powdered sugar mixture. Place in candy cups.

About 40

SUGARED PECANS

TAMMY RAYNES
NATCHITOCHES, LOUISIANA

2 cups sugar

1/4 cup water

1 teaspoon cinnamon

4 cups pecans

In large skillet, combine sugar, water and cinnamon; stir constantly over medium-high heat until sugar melts. Add pecans, stirring constantly until sugar begins to adhere to pecans. Remove immediately; spread on parchment paper. When dry, break apart and store in container.

About 3/4 pound

ALMOND BUTTER CRUNCH

MICHELLE HALL
CHESTER SPRINGS, PENNSYLVANIA

1 1/2 cups butter

2 cups sugar

1 lb. sliced almonds (about 5 cups)

2 cups semisweet chocolate chips (12 oz.)

1 In small saucepan, heat butter and sugar over low heat until melted. Reserve 1 cup almonds; stir in remaining almonds. Heat mixture until temperature reaches 310°F, stirring constantly. Pour mixture evenly into 13x9-inch pan.

2 In another small saucepan, heat chocolate over low heat until melted. Pour and spread melted chocolate evenly over almond mixture; sprinkle with remaining 1 cup almonds. Break into bite-size pieces when cool.

About 4 dozen

TERRIFIC TOFFEE

GWEN CAMPBELL
STERLING, VIRGINIA

1 1/4 cups chopped pecans

3/4 cup packed brown sugar

1/2 cup butter

1/2 cup semisweet chocolate chips (3 oz.)

Spray 8-inch square pan with nonstick cooking spray. Spread pecans in pan. Heat brown sugar and butter to a boil. Cook, stirring constantly, 7 minutes. Spread mixture evenly over pecans. Sprinkle chocolate chips over hot mixture; spread melted chocolate over candy. While hot, cut into 1 1/2-inch squares.

About 2 1/2 dozen

PEANUT BRITTLE

NANCY WIKE
HUDSONVILLE, WISCONSIN

2 cups sugar

1 cup light corn syrup

3/4 cup plus 2 tablespoons water

2 cups raw peanuts

3/4 cup butter

1 teaspoon vanilla

1/8 teaspoon salt

1 1/2 teaspoons baking soda

1 In large saucepan, mix sugar, syrup, and water; heat to 250°F. Add peanuts; cook to 290°F. Remove from heat; add butter and stir well. Return to heat; heat to 300°F. Remove from heat; add vanilla, salt and baking soda. Stir briskly until blended.

2 Pour immediately into 2 (13x9-inch) pans. Quickly spread until about 1/4 inch thick; cool. Break into pieces.

About 6 dozen

BUCKEYES

BUCKEYES

SUSAN KROUNGOLD
YOUNGSVILLE, LOUISIANA

1 cup softened butter

1 lb. creamy peanut butter

1½ (16-oz.) pkg. powdered sugar

1 (1-lb. 4-oz.) pkg. chocolate almond bark

1 Line baking sheet with parchment paper. Beat butter, peanut butter and sugar on medium speed until well blended. Roll into 1-inch balls. Place on baking sheet; refrigerate 30 minutes.

2 In small saucepan, melt chocolate over low heat. Dip each ball halfway into chocolate. Place on parchment paper to set.

About 7 dozen candies

CHOCOLATE TURTLES

VIVIAN NIKANOW
CHICAGO, ILLINOIS

1 (½-lb.) bag vanilla caramels

2 tablespoons heavy cream

1 teaspoon vanilla

1½ cups pecan pieces

1 cup semisweet chocolate chips (6 oz.), melted

1 Line 2 baking sheets with aluminum foil; spray with nonstick cooking spray.

2 In medium saucepan, combine caramels and cream. Melt caramels over low heat, stirring frequently. Remove pan from heat; add vanilla. Let mixture cool 10 minutes.

3 Arrange about 30 pecan mounds 1 inch apart on baking sheet. Spoon quarter-size dollops of melted caramel over pecan mounds. Let stand 30 minutes or until caramel mixture is firm. Spoon melted chocolate over caramel; cool about 1 hour or until chocolate is set.

About 30 turtles

VINCE'S GOOF BALLS

MRS. VINCENT ADAMS
HAMMOND, LOUISIANA

1 (14-oz.) can sweetened condensed milk

1 (16-oz.) pkg. powdered sugar

1 (14-oz.) bag flaked coconut

2 cups chopped pecans

10 (1-oz.) squares semisweet chocolate

1 tablespoon shortening

1 In large bowl, combine milk, powdered sugar, coconut and pecans. Work together with hands or spoon until well blended. Cover and refrigerate 3 hours. Roll into 1-inch balls. Arrange on baking sheet; cover and refrigerate at least 8 hours.

2 Line baking sheet with parchment paper. In small saucepan, melt chocolate and shortening over medium-low heat; remove from heat. Using toothpick or 2-tined fork, dip each ball in chocolate; let excess drip into saucepan. Place on baking sheet. Refrigerate in airtight container.

100 goof balls

COW PIES

TAMMY RAYNES
NATCHITOCHES, LOUISIANA

2 cups semisweet chocolate chips (12 oz.)

1 tablespoon shortening

½ cup raisins

½ cup chopped slivered almonds

In heavy saucepan, melt chocolate chips and shortening over medium-low heat; stir until smooth. Remove from heat; stir in raisins and almonds. Drop by tablespoonfuls onto parchment paper. Refrigerate until ready to serve.

2 dozen

GRANDY'S DIVINITY

MARY CHELETTE
MONTGOMERY, LOUISIANA

1/2 cup water

1/2 cup light corn syrup

2 cups sugar

2 egg whites

1 teaspoon vanilla

1/2 cup pecans

In medium saucepan, bring water, syrup and sugar to a boil over medium high heat. Cook until mixture reaches soft ball stage (240°F). Remove from heat; let cool 5 minutes. Add beaten egg whites and vanilla; beat until stiff peaks form. Add pecans. Drop from spoon onto parchment paper.

12 to 15 pieces

CHOCOLATE POPCORN BALLS

MARY STRONG
PLEASANTON, TEXAS

1/2 cup sugar

1/2 cup light corn syrup

1/4 cup butter

2 tablespoons unsweetened cocoa

8 cups popped popcorn

1 Heat sugar, syrup, butter and cocoa to a boil in large pot over medium heat, stirring constantly. Remove from heat. Stir in popcorn until coated. Cool to lukewarm.

2 Shape into 10 balls, dipping hands in cold water from time to time. Cool balls on parchment paper.

10 servings

MICROWAVE PEANUT BRITTLE

CLAUDIA WENDEL
FRESNO, CALIFORNIA

1 cup sugar

1/8 teaspoon salt

1/2 cup light corn syrup

1 cup raw Spanish peanuts

1 teaspoon vanilla

1 teaspoon butter

1 teaspoon baking soda

1 Spray 13x9-inch pan with nonstick cooking spray. In 1 1/2-quart microwave safe casserole, stir together sugar, salt and syrup. Stir in peanuts. Microwave on High 4 minutes. Stir. Microwave additional 4 minutes. Remove from microwave. Stir in vanilla and butter. Add baking soda (mixture will become foamy).

2 Immediately pour mixture into pan, spreading with two forks for thin brittle. Cool and break into serving pieces.

About 1 pound

WHITE CHOCOLATE FUDGE

DOROTHY H. JOHNSON
HECTOR, MINNESOTA

2 cups sugar

1 cup evaporated milk

$\frac{1}{2}$ cup butter

8 oz. chocolate almond bark, chopped (1 $\frac{1}{4}$ cups)

1 cup miniature marshmallows

$\frac{1}{2}$ cup flaked coconut

$\frac{1}{2}$ cup chopped toasted almonds

1 teaspoon vanilla

1 Spray medium saucepan and 10x6x1¾-inch pan with nonstick cooking spray. In medium bowl, combine sugar, milk and butter. Add to saucepan. Cook over medium heat until mixture reaches soft ball stage, stirring frequently. Remove from heat. Add almond bark and marshmallows; beat until melted. Quickly stir in coconut, almonds and vanilla.

2 Pour into pan. Refrigerate until set. Cut when cool. Garnish each piece with whole almond, if desired.

1 dozen

PEANUT CANDY BARS

VERONICA KENDRICK
LIBERTY HILL, TEXAS

$\frac{1}{2}$ cup butter

1 cup packed brown sugar

$\frac{1}{4}$ cup milk

2 cups powdered sugar

1 $\frac{1}{2}$ cups salted peanuts

In medium saucepan, melt butter over medium heat; stir in brown sugar. Cook over low heat 2 minutes. Add milk; heat to rolling boil. Cool. Add powdered sugar; beat until smooth. Stir in peanuts. Shape like candy bars and cool on parchment paper.

About 16 candy bars

PEANUT BUTTER POPCORN

CHRISTINA POOL
SALEM, OREGON

$\frac{1}{3}$ cup peanut butter

$\frac{1}{3}$ cup light corn syrup

$\frac{1}{3}$ cup butter

$\frac{1}{3}$ cup packed brown sugar

10 cups popped popcorn

In small saucepan, combine peanut butter, syrup, butter and brown sugar. Stir over low heat until blended and smooth. Pour over popcorn; stir until coated.

About 10 cups

CINNAMON CHOCOLATE FUDGE

MRS. GLENN CAIN
FORT SMITH, ARKANSAS

3 cups sugar

3/4 cup butter

2/3 cup evaporated milk

2 cups semisweet chocolate chips (12 oz.)

1 (7-oz.) jar marshmallow creme

1 teaspoon vanilla

1 1/2 teaspoons cinnamon

1 cup nuts (pecans, almonds or black walnuts)

Spray 13x9-inch pan with nonstick cooking spray. In medium saucepan, melt sugar with butter and milk. Bring to a boil 5 to 7 minutes or until mixture reaches soft ball stage. Remove from heat. Add chocolate chips, marshmallow creme, vanilla, cinnamon and nuts. Mix until well blended; pour mixture into pan. Cool completely. Cut into small squares.

About 6 dozen

PEPPERMINT STICK FUDGE

KAY SPARKMAN
ALEXANDRIA, VIRGINIA

1 (14-oz.) can sweetened condensed milk

2 tablespoons butter

2 1/2 cups white chocolate chips (14 oz.)

1/2 teaspoon peppermint extract

1 (16-oz.) bag peppermint candy, crushed (2 3/4 cups)

1 Line 8-inch square pan with aluminum foil.

2 In medium saucepan, stir milk and butter over medium-low heat until butter melts. Remove from heat; add chips, stirring until melted and smooth. Stir in peppermint extract and peppermint candy.

3 Spread mixture into pan. Refrigerate 8 hours or until firm enough to cut into small squares. Store airtight with parchment paper between layers.

About 2 dozen

PEANUT BUTTER FUDGE

TINA YOUNG
ATOKA, OKLAHOMA

2 cups sugar

3 tablespoons butter

1 cup half-and-half

1 cup miniature marshmallows

1/4 cup peanut butter

1 teaspoon vanilla

1 Spray 8-inch square pan with nonstick cooking spray. In medium saucepan, combine sugar, butter and half-and-half over medium heat. Cook and stir until mixture reaches soft ball stage. Add marshmallows, peanut butter and vanilla. Stir until marshmallows and peanut butter melt and are thoroughly blended.

2 Pour mixture into pan. Cool. Cut into 2-inch squares.

16 candies

CINNAMON CHOCOLATE FUDGE,
PEPPERMINT STICK FUDGE,
PEANUT BUTTER FUDGE

BUTTERSCOTCH FUDGE

TAMMY RAYNES
NATCHITOCHES, LOUISIANA

1 cup sugar

1 cup packed brown sugar

¾ cup sour cream

¼ cup butter

1 teaspoon vanilla

1 cup chopped pecans or walnuts

1 Spray 8-inch square pan with nonstick cooking spray. In large saucepan, combine sugar, brown sugar, sour cream and butter. Cook, stirring constantly, over medium-high heat until sugars dissolve and mixture comes to a boil.

2 Cook, covered, 2 to 3 minutes to wash down sugar crystals from sides of pan. Remove cover; cook until mixture reaches soft ball stage, stirring occasionally. Remove from heat; cool 30 minutes.

3 With wooden spoon, beat in vanilla until mixture thickens and begins to lose its gloss. Stir in pecans. Pour into pan. Cool completely. Cut into squares.

About 1¼ pounds

BUTTERY FINGERS

CLAUDIA WENDEL
FRESNO, CALIFORNIA

1 cup sugar

1 cup light corn syrup

1 cup peanut butter

3 cups corn flakes cereal

1 cup semisweet chocolate chips (6 oz.)

1 cup butterscotch chips (6 oz.)

1 Spray 13x9-inch pan with nonstick cooking spray. In small saucepan, heat sugar and syrup to a boil over medium heat; stir in peanut butter. Add cereal; mix well. Press mixture into pan.

2 In small saucepan, melt chips over low heat. Spread over mixture in pan. Cut and cool, or remove and break into free-form pieces.

About 4 dozen

ROCKY ROAD CANDY

CARLENE GOODEILL
CHICO, CALIFORNIA

1 (1-lb.) pkg. milk chocolate

1½ to 2 cups walnuts, pecans or macadamia nuts

1 (8-oz.) bag miniature marshmallows

1 Line baking sheet with parchment paper.

2 In large microwave-safe bowl, microwave chocolate on High until melted. Add nuts and marshmallows; mix well. Spread mixture on baking sheet. Refrigerate until set. Cut into squares.

About 2½ dozen

CHOCOLATE TRUFFLES

CATHY LEATHERWOOD
DALLAS, TEXAS

3/4 cup butter

3/4 cup unsweetened cocoa

1 (14-oz.) can sweetened condensed milk

1 tablespoon vanilla

Unsweetened cocoa or powdered sugar

1 In heavy saucepan, melt butter over low heat. Add cocoa; stir until smooth. Blend in milk. Cook, stirring constantly, about 4 minutes or until mixture is thick, smooth and glossy. Remove from heat; add vanilla. Refrigerate 3 to 4 hours or until firm.

2 Shape mixture into 1¼-inch balls. Roll in cocoa or powdered sugar. Refrigerate on parchment paper 1 to 2 hours or until firm. Store, covered, in refrigerator.

About 2 dozen

BRICKLE CRUNCH

STAN MISIOVSKI
DALE CITY, VIRGINIA

35 saltine crackers (1 sleeve of 16-oz. box)

1 cup butter

1 cup sugar

1 cup semisweet chocolate chips (6 oz.)

1 cup peanut butter chips (6 oz.)

1 Heat oven to 400°F. Line baking sheet with aluminum foil.

2 Place saltines on foil. In medium saucepan, melt butter. Add sugar; boil, stirring frequently, 2 to 3 minutes, or until sugar is completely dissolved. Pour mixture evenly over crackers. Bake 7 minutes. Sprinkle immediately with chips; spread to coat. Refrigerate 30 minutes or until hard. Break into pieces.

About 4 dozen

BEST-EVER PEANUT BUTTER BARS

GIGI MORGAN
INDIANAPOLIS, INDIANAPOLIS

11 graham crackers

1 cup butter

2 cups peanut butter

4 cups powdered sugar

2 cups semisweet chocolate chips (12 oz.)

1 Place graham crackers in large resealable plastic bag; seal bag. Crush with rolling pin.

2 In large microwave-safe bowl, microwave butter and peanut butter on High until almost smooth. Remove from heat; stir until completely melted. Add powdered sugar and graham-cracker crumbs; blend well.

3 Spread mixture into 13x9-inch pan. In small microwave-safe bowl, melt chocolate chips on High until almost melted; stir until completely smooth. Spread over mixture. Refrigerate just until chocolate is set. Cut into small squares. Store in refrigerator.

About 6 dozen

RECIPE INDEX

GENERAL INDEX

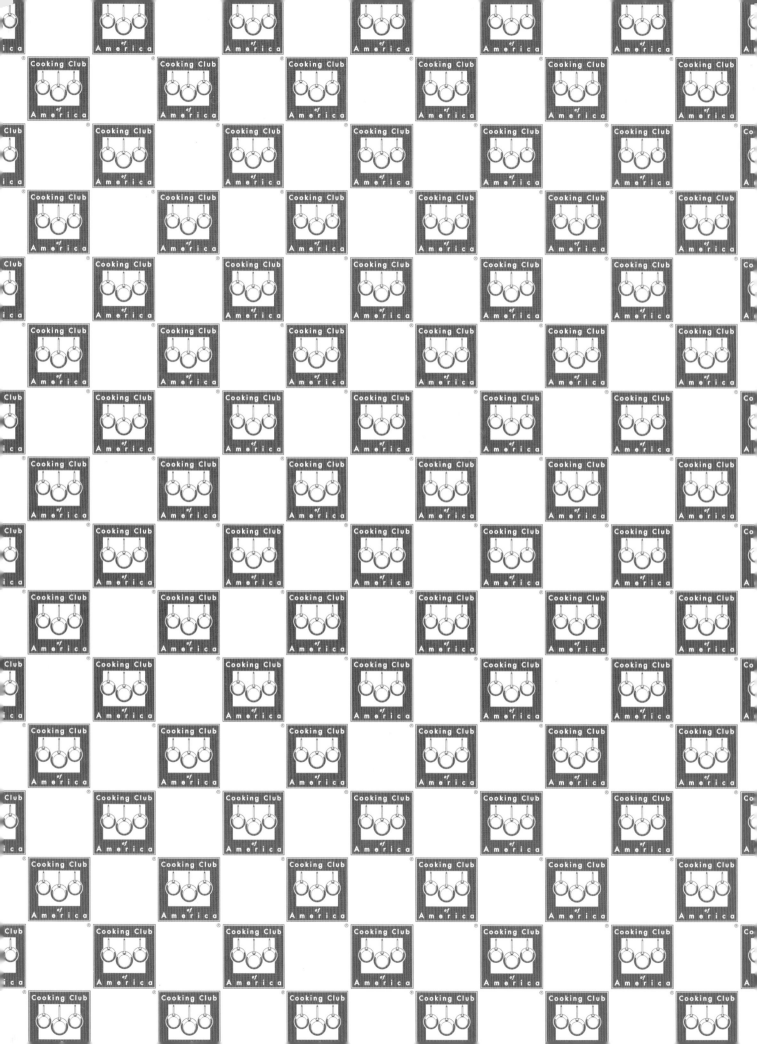